Flying Start

How to Make Your Own Luck at Work

NOTICED | SUPPORTED | PROMOTED

Carole Gillespie

Clink Street

London | New York

Published by Clink Street Publishing 2018

Copyright © 2018

First edition.

ISBN:
978-1-912562-25-1 - paperback
978-1-912562-26-8 - ebook

Carole grew up in a supportive but low-income family. Her parents left school at age thirteen, and she had no contacts or network to help her get started. She has always been curious about why people applying seemingly equal talent and effort often end up with very different levels of opportunity, success, recognition and reward.

Based on her experience over many years of building businesses and developing people, she has created The Relationship Code. It contains the six behaviours that build support, make you stand out from the crowd and attract unexpected opportunities through creating helpful lasting relationships. These can transform personal and business success. Anyone can apply the Relationship Code to create their own luck and success no matter where they start from, as Carole herself has proved.

For Suzi and Laura

Enjoy what you do. Do what you enjoy.

Contents

1. Making Your Own Luck _____ 3

2. Four Relationship Pillars _____ 9

3. Six Behaviours that Transform a Relationship _____ 35

4. Three Dimensions that Create Your Impact _____ 57

5. Building Your Brand Through Conversations _____ 61

6. Keeping the Conversation Going _____ 87

7. Protect and Enhance Your Brand _____ 93

8. What Next? _____ 103

Beyond the Relationship Code Foundation _____ 107

Q&A Index _____ 111

An Open Message from Your Current and Future Network of Contacts.

You may be the cleverest/most expert/quickest learner/most inspiring/most innovative person of your generation. You may have exactly the right style, enthusiasm and potential I need. But, if I don't know of you, or better still, know and have interacted with you several times, I have no way of knowing this.

Back in 2002, Donald Rumsfeld, the US Secretary for Defense, answered a question posed to him at the NATO HQ about the War on Terror. He explained his approach to taking decisions on this topic by talking about unknown unknowns, known unknowns and known knowns. In the context of networks, relationships and opportunities, if you are an unknown unknown, I have no idea of your existence. If you become a known unknown, I will know you exist, but won't know what you are capable of or whether I can trust you. If you become a known known, I may or may not have an opportunity for you today, but you'll certainly be on my mind when things change.

So, at every opportunity, just talk to the people you meet, get connected and stay in touch to become a known known whenever you can. Opportunities can come from the most surprising sources. Make it easy for me to know and remember that you exist. You never know when I will need someone like you.

Wishing you good luck and a great life. I hope to meet you some day.

1. Making Your Own Luck

As we enter the world of work, wouldn't it be great if we had continual support to stretch and develop ourselves? How amazing and fulfilling it would be if we could continue to learn, have access to a range of opportunities and avoid being trapped by any sort of 'glass ceiling'.

Many organisations will give you help with this, but to really stand out from the crowd and be lucky enough to get the best support and opportunities there are things you must do too – for the whole of your working life – starting now.

Your advantage is that you are going to find out what these are and, much more importantly, *how to do them* from the early days of your working life. Most people only start to appreciate what they are missing out on when they get to mid-career, *if at all.*

So, what is it that makes the difference that everyone can apply? The magic dust is the way you start and then continue the relationships you build with people in the business environment. Underpinning all that is the way you ask questions and have conversations.

"Is that all?" I hear you say. The answer is a resounding "Yes!" In this book I'll show you how to build a meaningful network no matter who you know now, how to reinforce your relationship with these people and how this can help you to get the opportunities you deserve. Best of all, you'll be able to do this in a way that feels natural and is welcomed by the people you meet.

Our Starting Point

Have you heard people say "It's not what you know, it's who you know"?

Maybe that was true in the past, when even knowing who was 'important' was difficult, let alone having a way to engage with them. It is true that some people still start off their life/career with the advantages of a ready-made network through parental or educational contacts. The difference now is that it is very easy for *anyone* to build their own network and level the playing field. In fact building *your own* network does more than this, it tilts the playing field *in your favour*.

No one is ever too young (or too old) to make contributions to their 'Relationship Bank Account'. The good news is that there are no restrictions on the amount you can invest or withdraw, or the time when you can do this. Whether you are a young entrepreneur, an undergraduate, an intern, a student on a holiday job, a school leaver, in an apprenticeship, on a graduate programme or simply in the early years of your working life, you must constantly be talking to people you meet and building your network. Why do this? Because your aim is to create and sustain positive relationships with these people to give both of you the confidence and understanding to potentially help each other now or in the future.

We will learn how to create positive and long-lasting relationships in the working environment (business relationships) and specifically how to make the most of every interaction. You'll be able to do this in a way that feels natural and which you can both enjoy. The result of this activity? You will stand out from the crowd and more people will be prepared to take the risk of giving you the chance to show what you can do – i.e. they'll take a chance on you.

This means more opportunities should come your way, more often. Your side of the bargain is that not only do you have to make the connections, but you have to keep them going. Read on and you will see how to do these things in a really effective way that will be appreciated by your connections. Great networks and great relationships don't happen by accident, they happen by design – consciously, confidently and consistently.

> *Relationship Reminder:*
>
> *Want someone to take a chance on you or your business?*
> *Build a relationship with them first.*

What's the Problem?

As I started writing this book, the term Generation Z had just been coined. This was defined as 17-24 year olds, who were just entering or had recently entered the workforce – some temporarily, some permanently. What was special about this group is that they were the first to have had digital technology at their fingertips from the day they were born.

Whilst this digital literacy is great for business operations, it does mean that people in this age group (and those that come into the workforce after them) have often had much less experience and variety in their non-digital (i.e. spoken) interactions with people.

In talking with people who are in the early years of their career or even just thinking about their future, I'm frequently asked four questions:

1. Starting a Conversation

"I'm really uncomfortable when I am in a group of people I don't know and tend to keep quiet and keep to myself. How can I make the most of these opportunities to meet people if I don't feel able to talk to them?"

2. Having a Meaningful Conversation

"Who'd want to talk to me? I'm at the 'bottom of the pile' and people are too important to spend time on me. How do I talk to more senior people to get myself noticed without looking like a creep?"

3. Building the Relationship

"I've got hundreds of friends on social media sites. It is easy to stay in touch with them individually or as a group. How do I do the same thing for people I meet related to work or my career?"

4. Using the Relationships

"It's all very well having a network and building good business relationships, but I've no idea how to make use of these. How do I use my network to help me progress in my career and get the opportunities I deserve?"

These are the fundamental questions (and more) this book sets out to answer for you.

I will do this by giving you a foundation for **understanding** relationships in business and an **explicit and practical approach** on how to create this foundation for yourself. I'll do this in three ways:

- A simple model of **Four Relationship Pillars™**. How to put them in place and how to judge the strength of relationships.

- A series of questions and answers (Q&As) throughout the book. These are questions on real life situations you are likely to encounter and advice on how to tackle them. They are all based on real questions I've been asked.

- An introduction to **The Relationship Code™**. The six behaviours that transform relationships. Apply these in both your personal and business life.

We will change the word *relationship* from something 'fluffy' and intangible to something that is easy to assess, and understand what happens when one of the Four Relationship Pillars is weak or missing. You will understand why the four components need to be place and be nurtured to enable you to increase your impact and open up unexpected opportunities for yourself.

So let's start by being clear that a *relationship* is simply:

The Sum of our Interactions

Nothing more. Nothing less. What this means is that every single interaction you have with someone changes the nature of your relationship. It might be a large impact or a miniscule one, but it will change it. That's true for both business and personal relationships. To say we have a relationship with someone does not tell us anything about the nature of that relationship. To say that one should build a business relationship is a meaningless statement. It is the nature of that relationship that matters and that relationship is built *one interaction at a time.*

For this reason, the focus in this book is on the interactions that happen both reactively and proactively. If we take care of the interactions, we take care of the *nature* of the relationships we build. The resulting network can make a real difference to our careers and lives now and in the future.

I like to think that this book has the potential to make you much 'luckier' in your career. One of the golfing greats, Gary Player once said, "The more I practice, the luckier I get." This applies in so many aspects of life. In your career, the more people you take the trouble to interact with and have meaningful conversations with, the luckier you will be. Whilst having conversations may or may not come naturally to you in a social context, it is important to learn how to have really great conversations in a business context. Practice mindfully and apply consciously and you should be one of the luckiest people around.

2. Four Relationship Pillars

It's very easy to be hard working and really good at what you do and still be 'unlucky' in terms of the way your career progresses and the opportunities that come your way. If we are going to have the motivation to start doing some things differently, we need to be really clear on why that change can give us a huge advantage. The advantage we need to create is one of having a positive personal **Business Brand**.

Think of any well-known brand, be it Netflix or Spotify or Snapchat. You'll have an immediate feeling about what these businesses are good at, what they stand for and how much you trust their services or products. No one from these organisations needs to be in the room with you to engender those feeling of confidence and appreciation. That's what you need to achieve on a personal level in your business world. That's what your Business Brand needs to achieve for you.

If there is an opportunity that could be right for you, you can't be invisible or an unknown quantity otherwise you won't even be considered or you will be too much of a risk. You need people in your network who will promote you, i.e. be your advocates when you are not around. We are talking about an army of supporters who are each able and willing to put their head above the parapet and argue for you to be given an opportunity to show what you can do. All new businesses have to start somewhere to build and then sustain their brand. You are no different, so let's get started.

Four Relationship Pillars

If we don't understand the four relationship pillars that can hold a strong 'relationship roof' over our head, how can we set about putting them in place? In this section, we are going to step into the mind of a person with whom you might want to build a business relationship and start to establish your Business Brand. Let's discover the Four Relationship Pillars by thinking about the five questions these people might be asking themselves about you.

Relationship Pillar 1: Your first pillar hinges on being visible.

> *Relationship Reminder:*
>
> *If you can't be seen, you can't be found.*

Here's the first question:

Do I Know You? Invisibility Cloaks

If people don't know you exist, they can't bring opportunities to you. It's not that they don't want to; it's just too difficult, unless you make it easy for them to do so by being visible and memorable.

We are all quite familiar with the visibility that comes within our social networks. Whether we use Facebook, Instagram or Snapchat or any of the many ways to interact on social media, we know it is an easy way to stay in touch, to remind people we exist and arrange to meet up. It's the natural thing to do.

For many people, starting out in their career or entering the world of work, the value of visibility gets forgotten, or it feels too hard to make it work. If the place you work is very hierarchical, maybe you feel it is not the 'done thing' to speak to people outside your area or higher up in the organisation. So, let's have a look at three types of invisibility cloaks that you and other people wear and let's see how we get rid of them and start to be seen properly.

Three types of cloaks:

1. The type you wear

2. The type other people wear

3. The type you think other people are wearing

Your Cloak

Recognise this? You are in a room with people you don't know – maybe a large room before a meeting. What do you do? Walk round and introduce yourself and chat to the people there. Or pull your invisibility cloak over your head and stay focused on your phone/tablet so you don't have to make possibly awkward conversation? What a waste.

Relationships in business are built one interaction at a time. If you don't have an interaction – don't even say "Hello" – your relationship with the people in that room can't start. That's a real missed opportunity for you … and them.

***

Q&A1: Starting without any contacts

I come from what is often described as a 'disadvantaged background'. I've been lucky enough to have supportive parents and get a good education and have recently started a decent job. I can't help noticing that many of my colleagues have a very different background to me. You know the type: parents are very senior in big businesses, the children have gone to the best schools and universities and through these have connections that seem to enable them to get access to anyone. The father of one of my colleagues is even a partner in the firm we both work for, and hence she already knows many of the leadership team here. How do I compete with that level of visibility when I have no worthwhile contacts to help me?

Lula

Lula,

We've all got to start somewhere. You just happen to be the first in your generation to have the opportunity to achieve real social mobility, just like me. You are very lucky to have the capability and support to enable you to have this amazing opportunity. So let's concentrate on what you can do, rather than your perception of what you might be up against. Control what you can control and don't waste time worrying, or worse, resenting, what you can't change.

As of today, it is true that you don't have a large network … yet. Let me ask you a question. How many new people have you met since you started your job? 1, 10, 50, 100? What did you do when you met these people?

Firstly, I hope you spoke to them and treated them with respect. Whether it was a cleaner, a messenger, a colleague, your boss or even your friend's father, they all deserve to be treated the same, i.e. treated the way you'd like to be treated if the situation were reversed. Each person should be treated as an intelligent adult doing a meaningful role. Each person working in your business will be doing something that is contributing to you having a job and ultimately your success. Remember that.

Let's assume for simplicity that everyone you've met is at the same level as yourself. That makes it very easy for you to talk to them as an equal and get to know them, their role and what they are working on, and, over time, what challenges they've got.

I'm now going to state the obvious. Each of the people you meet will get older, get more experienced and be meeting people that you don't know. Many of them will move to other organisations. Some, maybe yourself as well, will become very senior or start their own businesses. In 2, 5, 10, 20 years' time, your colleagues will increasingly be working around the world and be in a huge range of roles and organisations. It is not necessary to go out and make contact with very senior people in order to create a really helpful and worthwhile network. You can start simply by actively getting to know the people who are around you and who you meet as a natural part of doing your job. Learn what matters to them, be helpful and stay visible, and in the blink of an eye, you'll find your 'colleague network' has morphed into something spanning multiple professions and organisations.

I often talk about investing in a Relationship Bank Account. That's important whatever your start in life. Like many financial investments, the relationships you create early in your career and nurture over time, are often the ones that enable you to provide help and support to each other as you both progress in your careers. Best of all, if you stay in touch, you will have shared history which is much more powerful than a one step removed parental contact. You'll have a meaningful relationship that has stood the test of time and been valuable for both of you.

PS It sounds as if you could actually be privileged rather than 'disadvantaged'. You've started off with the intellect AND the parental support that's enabled you to get to a point where you have the opportunity to make the most of your talents and your life. Don't forget this. You may be surprised as you make friends with people from different backgrounds to yourself, to find out that they are in fact less privileged than you in the things that matter most. That's certainly what I've found.

***

Their Cloak

You're almost certainly not the only one who feels this way. Look up from your technology and look round the room in any situation where some people don't know each other. Instead of talking and getting to know people as they arrive, they are missing out too. You need to help each other. As a minimum you can get the conversation going by talking a little about how uncomfortable you find these situations. That should enable both of you to have common ground and allow you to take your cloaks off for a while and get at least one relationship out of the starting blocks.

***

Q&A2: Making 'small talk' comfortable and interesting

I'm really shy. I hate making forced small talk with people I don't know. It's much easier to avoid eye contact and pretend to be absorbed in something else. I know I ought to make the effort, but don't know how and I don't know what to say. How do I make the most of opportunities to get to know more people without feeling I am forcing myself on unwilling victims?

Yuki

Yuki,

Feeling that you are forcing a conversation on an unwilling or uninterested party is no fun. The trick is to make it as easy as possible for a person to respond to you. How do you do this? The answer is really simple; you ask a good question. A good question is one that the other person will be happy to answer AND gets a conversation going.

If you are in the same room as another person, the most natural question is something to do with the reason you are in the room together: e.g. a very simple, "Which area do you work for?" or "What are you hoping to get out of this meeting/conference/session?" is really easy to answer. This gives you some information about the person and then enables a second question, e.g. "Interesting, what are you working on at the moment?" or "Why's that important for you?"

Listen and learn.

However, before you ask your question, introduce yourself. How can you be known and remembered if the person you are talking to doesn't know who you are? Give it a go and see what happens.

***

Imagined Cloaks

Even people who are quite happy to speak to their peers for the first time often shy away from speaking to more senior people when they get the chance. "Why would they want to speak to me? I'm only the…" You'd be surprised how much many senior people enjoy speaking with people who are at the different levels in their organisation. In fact, it is the very senior ones that usually enjoy this most. You are imagining an invisibility cloak that often isn't there. They appreciate it when you approach them for a conversation. We'll learn how to do this later in the book. In the meantime, here's something to get you thinking…

***

Q&A3: Getting noticed in a crowd

I'm attending a roadshow next week that will be hosted by the top team in my company. I'll be in the room with quite a large number of my colleagues and of course the big bosses will be there. How do I get a relationship started with the people that lead the business I work in without it looking like I am trying to 'suck up' to them or be disrespectful?

Chung

Chung,

There's one thing you have to understand before I can answer this question. Here it is: people, no matter how senior, are just people. If they are particularly senior, they may be older or have deep expertise that you have yet to acquire … but they are still just people.

As someone who writes and speaks regularly, feedback is always appreciated. I mainly get that through being asked questions and conversations during and after an event. Without it, how can I answer my own big questions like whether people understand my messages and if they find them relevant to their lives; or the smaller questions of whether my slides are helpful?

So, to get back to answering your question: on the day, keep things simple and start by listening carefully to what each person has to say at the roadshow. What interests you about it? What would you like to know more about? Why? What observations do you have about what was said? Listen carefully and take some notes. Don't expect to be able to start a business relationship with these people unless you first find out what they are trying to achieve by really listening to what they say.

Then, formulate a question that means they have to think before they answer. That will start to get you noticed for the right reasons. At your roadshow, you can ask it in a Q&A session or you might get a chance to ask it directly during a coffee break. If you don't, nothing is stopping you dropping a note to the person to ask the question outside of the main event if it is something you'd like to know… and don't forget to introduce yourself before you ask your question.

***

Relationship Pillar 1

Pillar 1 is Knowing and Being Known.

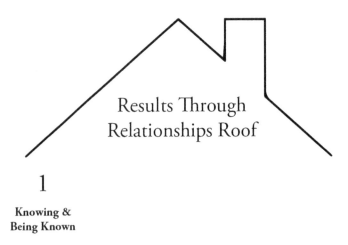

Think of our pillars as double strength pillars. It's you and another person linked together supporting each other.

What's the spectrum of Knowing and Being Known? It's all the way from a single quick hello or reading an article (or a book like this) to an 'always open door' where you will find time for each other no matter what else is going on. Wouldn't that be a great place to be with a whole range of people where you work and beyond?

This clearly doesn't happen straight away. It takes time and many interactions before two people really feel they know each other. Being Known is a funny thing. In the early days of Being Known, if you don't do things to make sure you are remembered, guess what? You'll get forgotten. So, when you make a contact and take the first step on that business relationship, you'll also need a way to have a second contact soon after. That doesn't need to be face to face, but it does need to happen.

Think again about your social media accounts. You make a new friend and posts and photos keep you remembered. The same principle applies in business; it just needs a little (not much) more effort than with your social networks.

***

Q&A 4: Following up after an event

I went to a Kick-Off meeting last week where most of the people in our organisation came together to hear about how we did last year and what the plans are for next year. It was very interesting and fortunately quite informal. I got to speak to people I'd not met before during the coffee breaks. I learnt quite a bit and met some nice people, some of them quite senior. How do I take advantage of the fact that I met new people who work in different areas to me?

Hana

Hana,

That's brilliant that you spoke to people across your organisation. Congratulations. You've taken the first step in Knowing and Being Known. Notice there are two parts:

If you are going to make the most of the effort you made, start now by writing down the names of each of the people you met and all the things you found out about them in your conversations (if you haven't already done that). This could range from the area they work in, which football team they support, what they are working on, where they went for their last holiday etc.

Next, within a couple of days, send them a short personal note/email/text depending on which format feels right.

For example, "It was interesting talking with you at the Kick-Off this week. I enjoyed our conversation on the work you are doing on setting up a scheme for apprentices to run alongside the graduate scheme. It sounds like it should increase the range of people who join us, which should be a good thing. Hope to meet you at other events from time to time and hear how the scheme is progressing, Hana."

or

"It was interesting talking to you at the Kick-Off last week. It sounds like you had an amazing trip travelling round South America. I'm hoping to do something similar in the next few years, so maybe I could get your advice nearer the time? Hope to meet you at other events from time to time, Hana."

Whatever you say, be honest and be yourself. Don't make things up. All you are doing is continuing the conversation remotely and demonstrating that you listened when you were together. What you are also doing is giving a nudge to the person's memory of you. They will probably have spoken to lots of people, but you'll probably be one of only a very few who follows up. That's a nice start to your business relationship. It is equally relevant for junior and senior people. Just make the note appropriate.

Your next task is to consider what you learnt and see if there is anything you can do to help them. Often that is just a snippet of information that they will appreciate. e.g. an interesting article on their area of interest or a congratulations on their team winning an important match. Do this in four to six weeks' time.

Get in the habit of keeping your eyes open for things other people will find helpful. But, you can't do that until you know and remember something about them. If you can't make your first note specific to them, you have not made the most of the conversation opportunities you had at the Kick-Off. It's even more of a waste if you did have some great conversations, but you can't remember who with or what was discussed. Write things down straight away when you get these opportunities, and ideally do it before you go on to the next conversation.

If you can do these two things, you will have got your new relationships off to a flying start and be remembered much more than most of the other people with whom they had conversations at the Kick-Off. There are other things you will need to do to keep it going, but unless you do these two, you'll be forgotten really quickly, if you haven't been already!

***

Knowing and Being Known is just one element of a relationship. Without it, there is no relationship at all. Even if you start a relationship, if you do nothing to keep it going, you will be forgotten and that means you are back to square one.

Let's move on to Pillar 2.

Relationship Pillar 2: Your second pillar hinges on your consistency.

Relationship Reminder:

"You are what you do, not what you say", or, to put it another way "Actions speak louder than words."

Here's the second question:

Can I Trust You? Snakes and Ladders

Not everyone you meet and start to get to Know is someone you want to be associated with. You may feel a person is not being honest with you, or they are 'only in it for themselves' or maybe they are taking credit for things you have achieved. In the business world there is much competition, but this doesn't mean you have to forget your personal integrity to get on. You do have to understand what behaviour inspires trust. You also need to have a strategy for working with people you can't trust without compromising your own integrity.

Your integrity is an integral part of your Business Brand.

Sometimes the people around you will demonstrate they can't be trusted.

***

Q&A5: Handling untrustworthy people

I have to work with a person I simply can't trust. He will tell me one thing and then I hear he has said something completely different when I'm not around. Also, he might agree to do something in a meeting and then renege as the deadline approaches and I end up having to do it. This is making my work life very difficult and causing me a lot of stress, as I simply can't rely on anything he says. I have no say over this person's role and have to keep working with him. How can I make our working relationship at least tolerable?

Amin

Amin,

You've learned very early on in your career the negative power of inconsistent behaviour. You've personally experienced how unsettling this is, especially when it also has the potential to make you look bad. This person is demonstrating the fastest way to create mistrust or destroy any trust that existed. If nothing else comes of this unpleasant learning experience, let it be that you don't fall into the same trap.

In terms of tackling the second problem, I have found two things to be helpful. The first is making sure that you have a visible record of what has been said or committed to and also to make it clear that you are not a fallback option. At present, it seems like there are no consequences of non-delivery for this person.

If we give the person the benefit of the doubt, maybe they forget what they have promised and/or they are insecure and like to say what the listener likes to hear. So, you have to help them avoid these two situations. This means a little more work for you initially, but it will be worth it. You'll need to explicitly agree what's been agreed and follow up before it is too late.

The next time you have a meeting or conversation where something is agreed, confirm what's agreed verbally while you are still together, write it down and then send a note to the person after the meeting with the details of the agreement. It is then up to them to deliver, or come back to you to say they disagree. Generally people will do what they say they will when there is tangible evidence that they made the commitment.

If they continue the pattern of behaviour, then you have the evidence to take more formal action. What you can't do is keep picking up the pieces when they fail to deliver. Having confirmed in writing the agreed expectations, don't leave it until the last minute to check on progress and reconfirm when they will deliver their part of the bargain. At least give them the opportunity to do what they said they would do.

Essentially all I am saying is that you need first of all to make sure that you really have reached a shared understanding about what the person will be doing and you also need to remind them if there is little evidence of progress.

In terms of saying things behind your back, don't let it bother you. You can't control what they say, but if you behave with integrity and can 'look anyone in the eye' in terms of your own behaviour, that's all you can do. Let others judge you by your actions.

***

Sometimes, the people around you will try to take advantage of you.

***

Q&A6: Saying "No"

I try to be helpful to the people I work with, both internally and externally. However, I'm beginning to feel that the things I do to help, which are outside of my main job, are now expected of me as standard. For example, while my colleague was on holiday, she asked me to do the monthly report for her. Since she returned, she's expecting me to do it every month because "You're really good at it," she says. The problem is it takes me a whole day to do and means I fall behind on my own responsibilities, which makes me look like I'm not pulling my weight. How do I get things back to how they should be and stop being taken advantage of?

Isaac

Isaac,

There is a fine line between being helpful and doing too much for other people. Being helpful is a really good trait to have. Most people will appreciate the help you give them and hopefully reciprocate. Being helpful is a great way to build a relationship … until it goes too far. It is up to you to stop that happening. If you have the capacity to help out a friend or colleague, by all means do so. But, you need a way to judge when saying "no" to a request is the right thing to do.

Here's a simple checklist for you:

1. *Do you have the capability to fulfil the request?*

2. *Do you have the capacity to fulfil the request without compromising commitments you have made elsewhere?*

3. *Is there a good reason to say yes?*

4. *Is this a one-off or is a regular commitment required?*

For a simple-to-do, one-off request for help we can all usually be flexible. The problem comes when our flexibility undermines our own performance, and hence our ability to deliver on our own commitments.

Let's examine your motivation for being ultra-helpful. Is it that you want to be liked? Is it that you want to be seen as indispensable? Is it just that you feel uncomfortable saying no? Work out what it is, then have a strategy for when and how to say yes and say no.

Use this model as the basis of your response: When a request comes in, take the time to decide what is the right answer for you. "Let me check whether I can do that properly for you. I'll get back to you later today."

Test the request against the four criteria above. Decide the answer and go back within the timescale you promised. "I've thought about your request and I'm not the best person to do it/I'd be happy to do it while you are on holiday as long as you can take back the responsibility immediately on your return/ I'd love to get involved in that with you."

If the answer is "no", try to help them get alternative help if you can. "I don't really have the knowledge you need, but Jane in accounts would probably have the right background. Do ask her."

Then agree what you think has been agreed. Even in a short conversation like this, people can end up with different understandings of the outcome.

In summary, of course be helpful when you can, but be clear in your own mind why you are saying "yes". The best way to avoid being taken advantage of is to say "no" at the right time and if you do say "yes", for you both to be clear on exactly what you are saying yes to. Then, do it enthusiastically and to the best of your ability. That's being really helpful.

***

Relationship Reminder:

A clear and confident "no" is better than a half-hearted "yes" or "maybe" which leaves the requester uncertain about what they can expect from you.

Provided you hold yourself to account on your promises, you have the right to expect others to do the same – irrespective of the level of seniority of the person.

***

Q&A7: Approaching senior people

During a recent meeting I attended, one of the senior people in the room said, "If you would like more information on this topic, just get in touch with me." As it happens, it would be really helpful for the project I'm on to get a better understanding of the overall aims of the project, rather than just the deliverables from my part. Do you think she really meant the offer or was it just a throwaway line? How do I find out and get the information from her that would be useful?

Nasrin

Nasrin,

You already know the answer to your question. You just ask. I assume that the only reason you are hesitating is because this is someone outside your normal contacts and/or very senior. No matter who the person is in your organisation, you have the right to expect that they will do what they promise. So, the only question is how you go back to them, not, whether you do.

Ideally, you would speak to the person immediately after their session/ presentation and ask them if you can take them up on their offer. Be ready with why this would be useful to you and them. Don't try to have the conversation offered immediately unless there is sufficient time to do so. Just get confirmation that it is a good thing to do and agree how it is going to get set up ... or better still, put a time in the calendar there and then.

If you can't do that (as speakers often have to dash away), a very short note is probably easiest. For example, "At the project meeting this week you said that you were happy for people to get in touch with you if further insight into the project would be useful. A conversation would be very helpful in putting my work in a broader context. In particular I'd like to understand X and Y better. If you are able to do this as offered, I would appreciate that. Thank you."

There is no need to go into detail, but you do need to give a reason why it would be helpful. Once you have the conversation set up, go along and enjoy it. The two of you have a shared interest so make the most of the conversation, but don't let your interaction end there.

After the discussion, make sure you send a short note letting the person know how the conversation helped you and what you gained from it. That will show the person that it was not a waste of their time.

You now have the opportunity to drop a note to the person from time to time. It could be about how what you learned has made a difference to how you have gone about your work, or simply that your project is complete and that you are moving on to a new project. Just make sure you stay in touch to stay remembered. You may even find you gain yourself a mentor as well as some useful information.

So get that meeting organised and, if something similar happens again, try to speak to the person immediately and get the date set up before they forget what they offered.

***

Relationship Pillar 2

Pillar 2 is Trusting and Being Trusted.

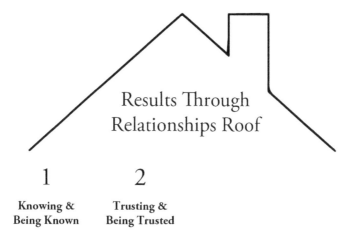

For a relationship to last, each person needs to trust the other.

Two things build Trust.

- Being Fair. A good test is whether you are 'doing as you would be done by'. If someone did to you what you are about to do to them, would it feel right to you?

- Being Consistent. Is your behaviour erratic? Are your principles unclear? Inconsistency in your behaviour leads people to be concerned that you cannot be relied upon.

In relationships, winning and losing trust is like the children's game of Snakes and Ladders. Seemingly small things can cause a significant jump, up or down, in the level of trust within a relationship. Let's suppose that someone comes to you with a complaint. That's going to be Snake, right? Not necessarily. If you can deal with it in a way that is fair to both parties and solves the problem, it can easily turn into a Ladder. That's because you have shown that you listened to the issue and found a sensible solution and did something that felt fair to both parties.

What impact do these first two Relationship Pillars have on your Business Brand? When you have built two strong pillars, they enable the person to answer the third question.

Do I have Confidence in You? Reputational Damage.

In the world of work, people don't go out of their way to help people they don't know and don't trust. What this means for you is that unless you have consciously built Pillars 1 and 2 with a variety of people, don't expect people to make the effort to support you. Why would they?

They don't know whether your actions/behaviour might undermine their own credibility if they do so. It is just too risky for them to take a chance on you.

Putting the Known and Trusted Pillars in place is all about making it much safer for them to be associated with you and to be willing to say out loud "Give this person a chance. They can be trusted to do what they say they will." That's a great start to your Business Brand.

We now know that we have to start conversations at every opportunity, stay visible thereafter and behave in a way that gives people the evidence that they can be confident in backing us.

But, backing us on what? In personal relationships, being known and trusted is sufficient for a great relationship. In the business environment, there needs to be more than this. There needs to be an explicit reason for an opportunity to come to us.

How do we find out what that is? Let's move on to Pillar 3.

Relationship Pillar 3: Your third pillar hinges on exchange of information.

> *Relationship Reminder:*
>
> *People judge you more by the questions you ask than the information you give.*

Here's the fourth question:

Do We Understand Each Other? Welcome to My World.

It's all very well knowing each other and thinking we are both good guys, but until there is something we can help each other with, then nothing more can happen. How do we get to that point? To start with, we need to understand what matters to the other person. If we don't know what matters to them, we can't help them. "But isn't this about them helping me?" you ask. That's a good question. The thing about business relationships is that they need to be founded on *mutual* understanding. A highly respected business guru from the 1970s, Steven Covey, had excellent advice on this matter. He said "Seek to understand before you seek to be understood." His book, *The 7 Habits of Highly Effective People* is still worth reading today.

In terms of building your relationship with a person you meet, it is simply taking the trouble to find out about them and what makes them tick. What are they trying to achieve? What's stopping them? In a social setting we do this naturally in the context of asking about family, friends, hobbies, etc. This is still nice to do in the work setting, but you will need a way to go beyond this and understand their world at work.

Good questions are the key to making this happen as they lead to meaningful conversations that enable you to understand each other. They are your most powerful tool for taking your Business Brand to the next level.

***

Q&A8: Asking great questions

I know that I am supposed to ask questions to get a conversation going. I get that. The problem is that when I ask them, I still don't seem to get into a proper conversation. What's the secret? How do I ask a question that gets people talking?

William

William,

What you've discovered is that all questions are not equal in their power to initiate a meaningful conversation. It took me a long time to get to grips with asking good questions. Asking good question takes real effort and concentration but it is worth it. Here's my approach to asking question. I hope you will find it useful.

I put questions into three categories:

Closed, Open and Ultra-Open. You've probably heard of open and closed questions before, but let me recap.

A closed question is one where the person is able to answer Yes or No, such as "Does this suit me?" They might not answer just Yes or No, but it is a reasonable and complete answer to give. In business you might hear a closed question such as "Shall we start the project on Monday?" or "Is Colin right for this role?" It is a question that invites making a choice and a decision. The power of this type of question comes at the end of a discussion or to bring something to a conclusion and agree an action. It is rarely a good way to initiate a conversation as it is gives a narrow base for discussion even if you get more than a Yes/No answer. In addition it puts the responder under pressure. How do you feel if someone asks you "Does this suit me?"

So what is a good way to open a conversation?

That's an open question. If I say that to you, you can't say Yes or No. You have to give me an answer of your own. You might say "I don't know, what do you think?" or you might say "I like to ask the person what they do for a living." Whatever you say, I can respond, and respond knowing a bit more about how you think. Either way, we can start making the conversation interesting to both of us.

As with many behaviours that are the basis for getting a conversation and hence a relationship going, it is much easier to ask a closed question than an open one. In a social setting we get away with closed questions because our friends help us out by giving more information than we have asked for. That happens less in a business setting because you haven't yet built up the trust to make this comfortable to do. There's a huge difference between saying "Shall we go ahead?" and "What are your thoughts about going ahead?" There's a time and place for each type of question.

My favourite type of conversation question is the one I call an ultra-open question. I define this as one where you don't 'lead the witness'. Let's suppose your favourite tennis player is Andy Murray and he has performed badly in a series of matches. I could say:

"Andy's playing really badly lately, isn't he?"

or

"Why is Andy playing so badly lately?"

or

"What do you think of Andy's recent performances?"

The first is closed and simply states your view. The second is open, but makes it explicit that you think he is playing badly, and the person will respond, but in that context. The third leaves the question totally open for you to hear the other's view.

If it is easier to formulate a closed question than an open one, it is definitely much easier to formulate an open question than an ultra-open one. It is really worth practising ultra-open questions, as the type of response you get will give you a fantastic start to your conversation.

This won't come naturally. I still need to concentrate to ask an ultra-open question. Here's what's helped me improve my ability to ask good questions. Find a friend/colleague who also wants to master the art of getting a good conversation going and practise together. Be 'mean' to each other. If one of you asks a closed question the only answer allowed is Yes or No. Nothing else. This will help you *both understand your own style of questioning and give you a safe place to try asking much better questions. You'll see the immediate difference in the way a conversation gets going and flows. How does that sound?*

***

Once you are in this sort of conversation, two things happen. The person will feel that you are genuinely interested in them (which you are), and you will start to understand them. They will want to know more about you and the process of mutual understanding gets going.

Relationship Pillar 3

Pillar 3 is Understanding and Being Understood

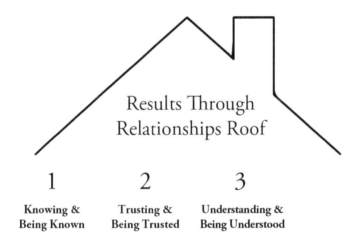

Results Through
Relationships Roof

1   2   3

Knowing &   **Trusting &**   **Understanding &**
Being Known   **Being Trusted**   **Being Understood**

If you don't understand the environment someone is in and the challenges they face, there is no way to relate to what they are trying to do, their motivations or goals. This is true whether you are talking to someone on the same training course as yourself or the head of your organisation. If you want to start to stand out, the early conversations are about them, not about you. This conversation style will start to set you apart, but it is what you do as a result of the Understanding you gain that is potentially the big prize for you and your new contact.

We now have three of our Four Relationship Pillars. Understanding is critically important, but it doesn't prompt action. Something can be understood and be interesting, but that's not the same as it being a catalyst for action. For that we need the Fourth Relationship Pillar.

Relationship Pillar 4: Your fourth pillar hinges on relevance

---

Relationship Reminder:

People need to discover for themselves whether you have something they need. You just need to make this easy for them.

Here's the fifth question:

Are You Relevant?
Show me you will make a difference to me.

You'll notice that we are still talking about the other person and not about you. We are now into trying to identify what value you can bring to the other person. From the understanding that you have gained in your earlier conversation, you should know what is important to them. If you can bring anything, no matter how small, which sheds light on these things, you will be helping them. That makes your input valuable because it is on something that matters to them. It's *relevant* information, rather than just more information in a noisy world. A relevant, helpful input or action is what will get you appreciated by the recipient and reinforce your Business Brand.

Relationship Pillar 4

Pillar 4 is Valuing and Being Valued

By understanding what matters to a person and then following up with something that helps address that important issue, you are building the Fourth Relationship Pillar. Value works both ways. In the early days of your career you may not know who will bring value to you. Just assume everyone has that potential. That's the beauty of contributing to your Relationship Bank Account from an early age. There's plenty of time to see how people behave, and adjust where you make the most effort.

More generally, in a relationship you can expect to get what you give. That's certainly true in the business world. If you are not being helpful and visible, you are unlikely to be found quickly even if you are highly talented and even then, you will be an unknown quantity. Consciously and consistently building all Four Pillars from the start of your career will enable you to create your Business Brand and give you a fantastic platform for keeping control of your destiny.

Recap: The Four Relationship Pillars

If we don't have a way to tell how good or bad a relationship is, it's very hard to set about changing it. We've begun with the Four Relationship Pillars. To have a relationship that works for both you and the other person, you need to:

KNOW | TRUST | UNDERSTAND | VALUE each other.

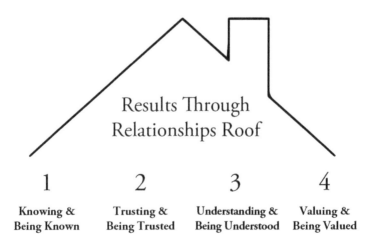

Results Through
Relationships Roof

1	2	3	4
Knowing & Being Known	Trusting & Being Trusted	Understanding & Being Understood	Valuing & Being Valued

Interestingly, the two words 'each other' are as important as the Four Pillars themselves. Remember they are double strength Pillars. When you first make a connection you are starting the process of Knowing each other. Over time this needs to evolve into remembering each other. For people to want to do this they have to feel that it is a worthwhile thing to do. That's where the other Pillars come in. When you have all four in place, it feels natural and safe to do things that help each other *and* you will both know what will have a real impact for the other. That's true whether it is between you and a person you work with, a client or with a senior person in your business. And yes, you can bring value to a senior person even if you are in a junior role.

In terms of the impact on your Business Brand, just being widely known and trusted will make you stand out from the crowd. Add in the dimensions of understood and valued and that's when your brand really takes off and you'll have people actively speaking up for you when you are not around. That's how you get really 'lucky'.

> *Relationship Reminder:*
>
> *A relationship is built one interaction at a time.*

3. Six Behaviours that Transform a Relationship

Knowing that the Four Relationship Pillars define the quality and effectiveness of each relationship gives us a way to judge its strength. Knowing that we need to build the four strong pillars of being mutually Known, Trusted, Understood and Valued doesn't tell us what behaviours create the pillars. To be able to invest in our Relationship Bank Account, and build our Business Brand we need to know what to do and how to do it. We need to understand what these behaviours are and how they build the Relationship Pillars. Six behaviours build strong relationship pillars. Together they make up The Relationship Code.

We will look first of all at the three most natural behaviours to adopt. These are the behaviours that build trust, start to get you known and keep you remembered. They are the ones that provide the foundation of your Business Brand.

Three Behaviours give a firm foundation to a Business Brand

- **Do As You Would Be Done By** – being fair and consistent (strengthens Trusted Pillar)

- **Always Truthful** – being honest and constructive (strengthens Trusted and Valued Pillars)

- **Always There** – being helpful and visible (strengthens Known, Understood & Valued Pillars)

Relationship Code Behaviour 1:
Do As You Would Be Done By

All I can do in this book is make you aware that following this principle will result in increasing trust and respect from the people you interact with. It is easy to break this rule when you are angry, on a tight deadline or have been let down.

Whether it is the call centre person speaking to you after a long time on hold, or a person who has just given you news you didn't want to hear, or someone has reneged on a promise, don't define your style by your instinctive response. I know I get frustrated when I'm kept on hold for 20 minutes and it is tempting and temporarily gratifying to take it out on the person who answers. But you know what, they don't deserve your anger. It's not their fault. Treat them fairly and with respect. You might be surprised how much more helpful people are when you treat them the way you'd like to be treated if the roles were reversed.

If this is important when you speak to someone you might not have to deal with again, just think how much more important it is with people within your own organisation or with clients.

Relationship Reminder:

People will forget what you said, but they will never forget how you made them feel.

If you can create a reputation, as part of your Business Brand, as someone who listens and tries to be fair you will start to build trust with the people you encounter. Being fair is not about being a 'soft touch'. Being fair is about finding reasonable responses to both issues and opportunities as they arise. Being fair is also a great basis for consistency of behaviour.

Some people only ever look out for number one. If your style is to get the best deal for yourself no matter the consequences to others, then you are probably not going to change your behaviour. You might feel that this modus operandi is the most effective strategy for you. Maybe it will be in the very short term, but it isn't a longer-term strategy for success in a world where everyone and everything is connected.

People will hear or see what you do so expect it to come back to bite you.

An African proverb says:

If you want to go fast, go alone. If you want to go far, go together.

In today's world, we can interpret this as being able to get away with selfish behaviour for so long, but your reputation will soon spread and it will become hard to get the support you need to make progress.

By treating others as you'd want to be treated yourself, you are taking people with you and building trust and respect … and laying the foundation for going much further and with greater support. The other impact of this style of behaviour is that it brings consistency to what you do and the way you do it. Trust is further enhanced when people are able to have confidence in how you will react to situations and that you do what you say you will do. The corollary to this is that you need to learn how to say "no" confidently and constructively if there is something you can't do. If you promise and then don't follow through that weakens the Trust Pillar.

***

Q&A9: Staying under control

I'm someone who finds it hard to keep my emotions under control. This is OK in a social setting and my friends know that I can be a rather volatile – reacting with great delight and enthusiasm when things go well and getting very cross or down when things go wrong. Now I am in a work environment, it would probably be a good idea for me to be able to present a calmer and more even temperament. Do you agree, or am I being untrue to myself if I try to do so? If you think I should change, how do I change my personality to behave in the way that is expected?

Charlotte

Charlotte,

It's OK to show your emotions at work. Just don't make other people feel uncomfortable or have them 'walking on eggshells' around you because they have no idea how you will react to anything. I think what we are talking about here, is you needing to be a bit more mature in your behaviour at work.

We expect children to react instinctively to situations they encounter – squealing with delight at something funny or having a tantrum if they don't get their own way. They are in their own world, conscious only of their own emotions and oblivious to the feelings of others. As we mature, we start to appreciate that we don't exist in a vacuum and that our actions have consequences for us and other people.

From what you describe about your behaviour with friends, it sounds like you might be a bit of a Drama Queen. My guess is that when things go wrong, it feels like the end of the world, it's always someone else's fault and you rely on your friends to listen to your grievances and help you get back to a more steady emotional state. If this is the case, watch out that you don't become too big a burden for your friends – people can only take so much angst.

So, even in a social setting, it's probably time to get a grip on your behaviour and its impact on others. You say it is your personality, but in reality, it is just a habit you've got into. Let's see how you might break that habit or at least tone it down.

In terms of the work environment, if you behave in the same volatile way at work as you do socially, what do you think it says about you? For a start, people will never know what to expect when they talk to you. Will you be in an angry mood because something has gone wrong, and will you take that anger out on them? Will you be feeling sorry for yourself because someone has let you down and hence be unwilling to engage fully with them to get things done? Will you be in a highly excited state and find it difficult to concentrate on important but more routine matters? None of these are good for you and your reputation or your relationship with others at work.

So you do need to break this habit. This isn't changing your personality, just giving you more insight into the impact of your behaviour and a way to direct your energies in a more helpful way. To answer your original question, yes, you should definitely be trying to be a calmer and more consistent person at work if for no other reason than it will make you a much easier person to work with.

For now, this is what to do each time you are about to react instinctively (like a child). Take a deep breath, pause and wait just two or three seconds before you respond. That will slow your heart rate and give you the time to put yourself in the shoes of the person you are about to react to. How would you want to be treated in a similar situation? What's a reasonable and productive way to react? Often, the very best thing to do is to try to understand more about the situation before you react. Asking a question shows you have listened to the initial information and gives confidence that you are going to behave in an adult fashion.

For example, if someone says to you "I'm sorry Charlotte, you're not going to be able to be part of the new Cyber Security project team despite our conversation the other day," there is an enormous difference between maybe crying and/or ranting about how unfair this is, and asking constructive questions such as "What's changed since last week; what other opportunities will there be in this space; what do I need to do to join the team for phase 2…" You'll still be disappointed, but you will have behaved appropriately and you'll have some information that will enable you to get yourself ready for the next opportunity. Maybe the person will even change their mind.

I also suggest you try this approach with your friends. If something goes wrong in your life, try asking for advice from your friends rather than just using them as people to share your self-pity.

Going back to the work environment, do be yourself, but also try to be more composed. People must be able to trust you to behave like an adult. You'll be surprised how helpful and understanding people can be when you are too.

Note: If you are interested in learning more about one psychological model of how people interact depending on whether they are 'playing' the role of an adult, a parent or a child then check out the book I'm OK. You're OK. *It was written in 1969 by Thomas A Harris and is based on the ideas of Transactional Analysis created by Dr Eric Berne.*

***

Relationship Code Behaviour 2: Always There

Particularly in the first six months of a relationship, it is easy for you to be forgotten unless there are regular reminders of your existence (and hopefully value). We now have many ways to do this. Whilst most relationships in business start with a face-to-face interaction, the *helpful* reminders of our existence can come through multiple media types. All interactions, be they email, text, etc., count *as long as* whatever you send or say is helpful to the other person.

This might sound onerous, and some of it does have to be highly personalised, but often it can be sent to multiple people. This is how you become increasingly well known with each of the people you've met.

***

Q&A10: Developing a business relationship after the first conversation

I was introduced to the new team leader the other day when I was on a client site. We hit it off immediately from a business perspective. We didn't talk for long, but seem to have similar views about things that might make our services better for our clients. I'm not sure what to do next. I'm unlikely to visit the site again for quite a while, but it just feels as if we could help each other and build a good business relationship. I just don't know what will feel right. How do I develop this as a business relationship in a comfortable and appropriate way?

Maria

Maria,

You don't say whether this person is male or female and I'm wondering if you feel that building a business relationship with this person could be misinterpreted. Don't worry about that, there are ways to maintain contact that are friendly and helpful without implying something more. More importantly, don't miss out on the opportunity to come up with some interesting business suggestions that could get you both noticed.

Firstly, capture the essence of your conversation. Be clear in your own head on the topics discussed, the issues the two of you identified and the initial thoughts you shared on tackling them. Now decide if by working on this together you might both be able to achieve something meaningful. Alternatively would a further conversation be helpful and interesting, but unlikely to have a meaningful impact. This will help you decide how to frame what you say next.

As a minimum, you need to do the following to build and sustain your new business relationship:

1. *Get back in touch. Send a friendly note summarising in a few words your shared conversation. To keep it simple, distil the three (or less) main points that came out of the conversation, e.g. "When we spoke the other day we identified two main things that if they could be changed, would make the delivery of our services much more efficient. They were the process for requesting changes and the numbers of review meetings. If it would be helpful to get back together for an informal conversation to work on how we might make this happen, I'd be happy to do this with you. Please get in touch if you'd like to do this."*

2. *If you wanted to be more proactive, you could end like this as an alternative: "I'll give you a call tomorrow to see what can work for both of us."*

In both notes, you are being helpful and reinforcing the initial conversation and your image. In the first, you are putting the onus on the other person to act. That's a good way to see how important they feel the issue is. However, if you feel the opportunity warrants your proactive attention, then keep control of the pace of the interaction. It's your choice. If you make a commitment or an offer make sure you hold up your side of the bargain. Never promise what you can't deliver.

3. *Let's now assume that you've had a second conversation and it turns out that there are good reasons why the initial ideas are unlikely to work, and you decide together not to take them any further. Does that mean you should stop any interaction with each other? No it doesn't. You've got the business relationship going, so with your new knowledge of the team leader's role and what that area is trying to achieve, you now know what they might find helpful.*

Make sure that you do one of these types of things every one or two months: drop a note re progress, send something that you've seen/heard of interest and say hello next time you are on site.

If your initial conversation had led to some form of working together, your business relationship would have developed naturally. When there is no specific reason to work together, that's the time to make sure you stay in touch helpfully … until there is something that you can do together.

That way you won't get forgotten and it will feel like you are always there for the other person.

***

Business relationships do sometimes develop into friendships. I have some wonderful friends that I met through doing business with various companies over the years. It is one of the great things about proactively talking to people – you get to know some great people. Just make sure that your behaviour in the business context is not compromised by your personal relationship.

Relationship Code Behaviour 3: Always Truthful

I hope that you wouldn't lie to your colleagues or clients on things that matter to them, e.g. "I'll have it finished on Friday", when there is absolutely no chance that this will happen. Having this type of difficult conversation is a real skill.

***

Q&A11: Giving difficult messages

I've got some information to give to my team leader about why I will not be able to deliver something I promised. There are good reasons why this is the case, but I'm worried I will end up taking the blame for something that I had no control over. How do I make the best of a really bad situation? I'm really worried about what will happen when I make the information known.

Hazel

Hazel,

You don't say how bad your bad news is, but you are clearly very worried about what will happen when you make it known. That's natural. What's also natural but very unhelpful is that people often take a long time to pluck up the courage to give bad news. All this does is reduce the options for finding a solution or a way to mitigate the impact.

How you give the bad news can have a significant impact on how it is received. Long, complex explanations before you get to the crunch point are not likely to help you or the listener. You need to stay in control of the conversation and make it as easy to follow and as constructive as possible. There is one thing you must do before you have the conversation and that is to have at least one recommendation on a course of action. You must show that you are being proactive and being part of the solution, not just of the problem.

A good 'giving bad news' conversation has four parts:

1. *Let the person know you have something to tell them that they won't want to hear.*

2. *Tell them in one sentence the issue you've faced and then in the second sentence what this means for them, e.g. "I've not been able get the final critical pieces of information for the report for HR as the person who can provide that information has not been available to provide it. We will need to let them know it won't be ready in final form by Friday." Wait for a response.*

3. *Be ready with a view on what happen next, e.g. "I can issue the report on Friday with part of the analysis missing and complete it when the information is available. At present I'm not able to confirm when that would be. Once I have the information I estimate that I will need two days to do the remaining analysis and incorporate the findings in the report ready for it to be reissued."*

Whilst the person may be angry/upset at this, it will be much worse if you wait until the Friday morning to break the news. At least now, there is a chance to speak to the client and set new expectations and give them a chance to adjust plans too (or speed up the provision of the missing information).

4. *Agree the course of action and, explicitly, who is to do what and by when. Make sure that what is agreed is genuinely possible, rather than an easy way out for the time being, i.e. don't agree to finish the report by next Friday if there is no way of knowing if you will have the information. Write down what's agreed and confirm it in a short note after the meeting. Then, absolutely make sure that you deliver on the agreement.*

Interestingly, sorting out a problem together can actually enhance relationships, provided you have been honest and step up to the mark to fix things.

Get prepared and go have that conversation today. Good luck.

***

However, what about when you end up having made a commitment to two people at the same time and now have a diary clash? I understand that it can be embarrassing to have to go to one of them and rearrange. It's not unusual for people to avoid this by calling to say they are sick instead. OK, you may not get found out; but what if you are? Suppose someone sees you in your first meeting at the time you were supposed to be meeting them? Now, that is really embarrassing. It may have only been a little thing in your eyes, but it leaves the other person wondering "What else are they lying to me about?" That's not a good place for your on-going relationship. Why risk it? Be honest and constructive about the meeting you have to rearrange.

More generally, just remember to apply these three Relationship Code foundation behaviours:

- **Do As You Would Be Done By** – being fair and consistent (strengthens Trusted Pillar)

- **Always Truthful** – being honest and constructive (strengthens Trusted and Valued Pillars)

- **Always There** – being helpful and visible (strengthens Known, Understood and Valued Pillars)

You'll find that establishing the foundation of your Business Brand is not difficult as long as you are conscious of these behaviours and the impact they have. You don't need new skills, just the understanding and motivation to behave in this way. After all, whether we've realised it or not, these are the very behaviours that build long term positive relationships with friends and family. Try observing your social and business interactions and make a point of using the approach. You may find you can change/rebuild difficult relationships and reinforce the good ones. Try it. What have you got to lose?

Three Behaviours differentiate and reinforce your Business Brand

This is where the hard work starts. These behaviours are not difficult to understand and pretty obvious once stated. The issue is that our natural behaviour is to do the opposite because it takes so much less conscious effort. Here they are:

- **Ask and Listen More. Tell Less** – being interested and interesting (strengthens Known, Understood & Valued Pillars)

- **Their Context Not Yours** – being relevant and understood (strengthens Understood and Valued Pillars)

- **Agree Expectations and Act On Them** – being specific and explicit (strengthens Trusted, Understood and Valued Pillars)

How hard can that be? In reality, unless you know how to do this and practise the behaviours consciously, it can be hard to do. You'll slip back into old habits quickly. You have been warned.

Relationship Code Behaviour 4: Ask and Listen More. Tell Less.

Whenever you are speaking to someone, you need to have a conversation, NOT a monologue. If you are doing all the talking, how can you possibly find out anything about the person you are with?

Whether someone asks you "What do you do?" or " How's your project going?" you need to give a small amount of information that paints a useful picture and then ask a question back. That's the start of your conversation. Typically people fall into one of two camps – either giving far more information than the receiver can cope with (or is probably interested in) or an unhelpful "OK" response. Neither makes it easy for you both to get talking.

***

Q&A12: Communicating succinctly

I've just started my own business and I'm so excited about what the new app I've designed enables people to do. Even though I say it myself, it is awesome. It will give people absolute control over their weight and it uses this new technique that's been developed by a psychology professor at Oxford University. It uses both AI and IA techniques and knows what your body needs without you even having to know yourself. The problem is I'm having difficulty convincing people that they should invest in it so I can take it from the pilot stage (which has been a great success) to full functionality and a complete, live product. How do I get people to understand what an amazing opportunity this is for them?

Faisal

Faisal,

Whilst you've given me a lot of information above, I still have no idea what your new app does. More importantly, I've no way to judge what, if any, impact your app would have on my life if I used it. I suspect that that is how the potential investors feel after they have listened to you. You probably give a lot of information (all of which makes absolute sense to you), without taking the time to understand either what matters to them or what mental picture they are forming of you and your product.

What's not in doubt is your enthusiasm for what you are doing and your commitment to it. Please don't lose that. However, if you don't make it really, really easy for the person you are speaking to, to grasp the power of your app in the first few seconds, you are unlikely to get or keep their attention. When you are in a situation where you want to get to point of mutual understanding and agreement, you have to do it by a conversation, not a monologue. That means you need to learn how to give a lot less, but much more helpful, information and also how to get feedback during the conversation, i.e. you need to ask more questions and listen to the answers, and give a lot less information.

Let me make the assumption that what your app does is enable people to lose the weight they need to lose without doing anything except listen to some tunes on your app. If this were the case, the fundamental information that you would need to impart right at the start of a conversation is this:

"My app enables people to lose the weight they need to lose by just listening to the tunes on my app. This means it is a way to solve the obesity problem for individuals and nations, saving lives and millions in healthcare costs."

That should get a conversation going! Be ready with an example.

"By listening to my app for five minutes each day and changing nothing else about their lives, my ten volunteers lost on average a stone each in a month."

The structure you need to use is this:

1. What is it you enable people to do (in one sentence)?

2. Why does this matter (in one sentence)?

3. Short proof example.

You'll notice that I've said nothing about Oxford professors or artificial intelligence. None of this is relevant until you've communicated the outcome and why it matters. Until your audience understands and agrees that this is important, there is no point going further.

The three sentences above are all you need to get the conversation going. Now get immediate feedback. Ask a question and be quiet while it is answered.

"What do you think the market potential is for an app that achieves this?"

The person you are speaking to now has a clear picture in their head of what is possible with your app and is having to consider for themselves how valuable it might be. If they see the value then, you have a very good chance that they will become an investor. If not, you have a chance to clarify any misunderstandings.

If you start off as above, don't lapse into massive detail at the first opportunity. Keep the dialogue going with small, relevant pieces of information and questions that really make the other person think about what they have heard.

Bring the conversation to a conclusion with a summary and a question: "You've told me you think this app could attract 100 million users. What are your thoughts about investing in my business?"

If you work on communicating only the information people need to make a decision, and you test their understanding and appreciation of what you have at each stage in the conversation, I'm sure you will find it much easier to get investors for your app.

Send me a link when it is live please.

Wishing you every success with your business venture.

***

As individuals, our brains are lazy. If we hear something we jump to conclusions. In the caveman/woman world making quick decisions based on past experience saved lives. Today, it prevents us listening properly to information we are given. If I start of by telling you that I have a Maths degree and I am a Fellow of the British Computer Society, you'll label me as a techie. If I start off by telling you I have my own business and I've sold hundreds of millions of pounds worth of services in my career, you'll have a different picture. Take great care with the first things you say. People will jump to conclusions whether they are conscious of it or not.

Relationship Code Behaviour 5: Their Context Not Yours

This behaviour is easy to say and very hard to do. Our natural inclination and simplest perspective is our own. How often do we say things like "I'd love to come and speak to you …", "I think you would enjoy …", "I know you would find this really interesting …" The thing is, if you are speaking to people (or emailing them), they don't care what you want. Also, you have no idea what they would enjoy or find really interesting.

When you are interacting with people by whatever medium, they just want to know if you have anything to say that is relevant to them (do you understand them and can you bring something they value?). You need to retrain your thinking, speaking and writing to make it easy for your audience to see for themselves why what you do matters to them.

***

Q&A13: Expressing value to the other person

I'm on an internship for six months with a creative company. I've told my boss that I'd love to be able to get out and meet clients and talk to them. However, I'm stuck in the office being given the boring bits of assignments and frankly, I'm not learning or contributing very much. It feels such a waste. How do I get more from my internship and at the same time give more back to the organisation that has given me this work experience opportunity?

Kaito

Kaito,

In your note you tell me what you want, i.e. "I'd love to be able to get out and meet clients and talk to them." So what? That's good for you, but what's in it for your employer? What would be a good thing for your creative company? Let's think about restating this in a way that shows a value to your organisation. That will give you a much better chance of achieving your goals and doing something that helps your organisation. What about:

"I've read that client X has a major investment in apprentice schemes. By including me in the team that visits them, we can show our own commitment to bringing on junior talent. That could set us apart from our competitors…"

or

"Client Y has Japanese ownership. As I am fluent in this language, maybe I can reinforce the genuinely international nature of our firm and build rapport with the local team through our common language…"

It actually doesn't matter what the reason is, it just has to be something that matters to the person you are talking to, not just to you.

If you take the trouble to think through what is important to the other person, and describe things from their point of view, your requests/arguments/input will be much more easily understood, recognised and acted upon.

So go back to the drawing board and work out why it would be good for your boss and the organisation for you to meet clients and talk to them. Then try your request again from their perspective rather than yours. It won't always work, but your chances of success will be much higher.

***

Relationship Code Behaviour 6:
Agree Expectations and Act on Them

So many things go wrong in relationships because people misunderstand what the other person wants and how important these things are. Everyone has got this wrong at some time and knows that the consequences can be horrible: annoyance, anger, irritation, incomprehension. That's just in the social setting where it ought to be fairly easy. In a business context there is even more opportunity to get things wrong and more wide ranging potential consequences for doing so. Finding out explicitly what is expected, challenging it if it is unreasonable, understanding its priority and then delivering the outcome needed is fundamental to building mutual understanding and value.

***

Q&A14: Getting clarity on expectations

I've been at my first company for six months and I still don't really know what I am supposed to be doing or how I can know if I'm doing a good job. It is really difficult to get any time to speak to my boss as he is always very busy. He gives me what feels like a random collection of things to do which are generally very easy and certainly require none of my qualifications. Almost anyone could do this job. That said, I like my colleagues and I really like what my company does. It makes a real difference in the world.

I am so bored and frustrated I am thinking that I need to start looking for a new job. How can I fix this situation so I don't have to move?

Rob

Rob,

Given what you say about your colleagues and the nature of the company you work for, it would be a shame to have to move. Here are two questions for you: 1. How many times have you tried to raise your concerns with your boss? 2. Did your boss have any warning that you wanted to have that conversation?

If your answer to the first question is none, then what do you expect? Your boss probably thinks you are quite happy and, I guess, is pleased that he has someone as competent as you to handle a wide range of tasks. It sounds like you turn them round quickly as they are so easy for you and this is probably making his life much easier than before you arrived.

If your answer to the first question is one or more, but you didn't warn your boss that you needed the conversation, I can see how a very busy person might not be able to address your concerns when they come up out of the blue. He should really be making time, but quite often the urgent overtakes the important when time is tight.

Let's look at the best way to get the conversation to happen. For those people who are ultra-busy (which can often also mean disorganised) you need to help them be ready and able to speak with you. This means getting a date and time in their calendar, along with a clear statement of the outcome needed and why this will help you and them.

So, at the end of your next conversation with your boss, just add in a BTW line such as "You know I've been here six months now and learned a lot about the company in that time. May I put some time in the diary to talk specifically about what you were expecting from me, what you'd ideally like from me in the next six months and maybe how we can make more use of my skills?"

That's short and to the point. You don't need to say anything else. Wait for the answer to your question. You'll either get a "yes", in which case put it in the calendar immediately, or you'll get a clarification question – "Why do you want to do that? Is something wrong?" Keep your answer very short. Unless you know they have time for the full conversation there and then (and you are prepared for it), just say "I know I can now do more than I'm doing and it feels the right time to refine the way we work together. When would you like to talk?"

Either way, you should get a time-slot to talk. You are most unlikely to get "no" as an answer. If you do get a "no", then you might be right about looking for another job. Any leader should be pleased to be approached by someone wanting to make a greater contribution.

Your preparation is then about how to structure the conversation to keep control. Start by putting together a short note that can go to your boss a few days before the meeting. For example:

Subject: Conversation with Rob

In readiness for our conversation this week, I've put together five questions that should help us get clear on what I should focus on and the results that would be most helpful to you. Here they are:

What were you expecting when I joined the team?

What aspect of that was most important and how am I doing so far?

What is going to be important for you for the next 6–12 months?

What is the best way for me to support you in achieving that?

How will we be able to tell whether I'm making a real impact for you?

Hope that is helpful. I'll see you at 4:30pm on Thursday in your office. Rob

This does two things. It reminds the person why you are having the meeting and it makes it easy for them to turn up to what should be a productive meeting, without having to do a lot of work themselves.

When you go for your conversation, take the note with you and confirm at the start that together you'll try to answer the five questions. If the conversation strays, it gives you a way to bring it back to the objectives of the meeting. Make sure you write down what is agreed and send a succinct summary note to your boss afterwards. You've now both got a record of what was agreed and a basis for challenge and tuning as things change.

Repeat in six months to capture what has changed.

In summary, all you are doing here is enabling your boss to articulate what he wants to achieve, your role in doing that and how you will both know you are successful. You might find that you end up with a much more demanding role, but it sounds like this is what you want.

What this conversation does mean is that there will be clarity on what you have to achieve, so make sure you achieve it. Go for it.

Note: In this type of situation, some people will say, "I can't talk to my boss like that!" I say "Yes you can." There is nothing that says you can't be assertive and make it easy for your boss to do the right thing – in this case have a conversation about expectations and priorities. Just be polite and show that it will be as helpful to them as you. Be brave.

***

> *Relationship Reminder:*
>
> *Silent expectations are the time bombs in relationships.*

So there we have it. The six behaviours that make up the Relationship Code.

1. **Do As You Would Be Done By** – being fair and consistent (strengthens Trusted Pillar)

2. **Always Truthful** – being honest and constructive (strengthens Trusted and Valued Pillars)

3. **Always There** – being helpful and visible (strengthens Known, Understood & Valued Pillars)

4. **Ask and Listen More. Tell Less** – being interested and interesting (strengthens Known, Understood & Valued Pillars)

5. **Their Context Not Yours** – being relevant and understood (strengthens Understood and Valued Pillars)

6. **Agree Expectations and Act On Them** – being specific and explicit (strengthens Trusted, Understood and Valued Pillars)

If you can adopt all six behaviours you will create more contacts that remember you and have the confidence to start to support you and speak up for you.

Adopting all six in one go is difficult. Adopting any new behaviour is challenging. Whether it's changing your diet or exercise regime to lose weight or enhance well-being, or taking the time to learn a new language, habits need to be embedded.

As you try to adopt the six behaviours that make up the Relationship Code, take one step at a time. It can take a long time for a behaviour to change to one that we do consciously and consistently. The two hardest to master (but the most powerful) are Behaviours 4 and 5: 'Ask and Listen More. Tell Less' and 'Their Context Not Yours'.

I recommend that you pick one of the behaviours at a time and practise applying it consciously in every situation you encounter. If you pick the ones above, you will probably need to work on them consciously for a month. In particular, it is very helpful to practise with a friend.

Most people hate role-plays. However, having the "What do you do?" conversation out loud and helping each other to get off to a really interesting start to this conversation pays dividends.

Now, before you continue, please make sure you are comfortable with the Four Relationship Pillars™:

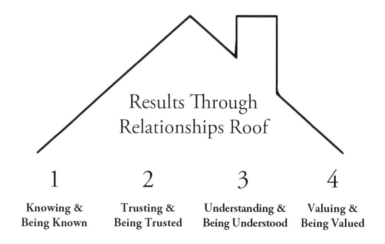

and the Six Relationship Code™ Behaviours:

**Do as you
would be done by**

Being fair
and consistent

**Always
there**

**Ask and listen
more. Tell less.**

Being helpful
and visible

Being interested
and interesting

**Known

Trusted

Understood

Valued**

**Always
truthful**

**Agree
expectations,
and act on them**

Being honest
and constructive

Being specific
and explicit

**Their context
not yours**

Being relevant
and understood

The Relationship Code
© Carole Gillespie at PbfP Limited

as they are the foundation for all that follows and are your passport to more support and fewer barriers in your career.

4. Three Dimensions that Create Your Impact

We all want to make an impact. During the Foundation Years of our working life, the main way we are usually judged is by what we know. That's typically what we are paid for – applying what we know. If we are poor at the things we are paid to do, we won't get far and may get attention, but not the type we want. But even early on, the impact we make can be enhanced (or reduced) by how we behave and by our ability to turn to others for support and guidance.

Three dimensions create your overall impact:

- **Your professional skills and experience:** What you know

- **Your relationships skills and tools:** What you do and how you do it; what you say and how you say it

- **Your professional connections:** Who you know and who knows you

i.e. Your KNOWLEDGE | BEHAVIOUR | NETWORK

They are all important to put in place and the relative importance changes as you progress through your career. What we are doing in this book is giving you the ability to get a decisive head start on your relationship skills and tools, and the breadth and depth of your professional connections. As these are going to become increasingly important as you progress, you'll be well ahead of the pack if you consciously build these skills, tools and connections ahead of others. My personal experience tells me that by the time you are in your late twenties or early thirties, the percentage of your impact from what you know could have dropped from around 65% to less than 50%. Why is that?

It's because more and more of your impact comes from the other two dimensions as you progress through your Foundation Years, on to your Breakthrough Years and then to your Leadership Years. Here's what I've observed in terms of how the source of one's impact changes.

Relative Importance of the Three Dimensions

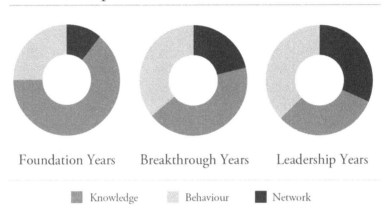

Foundation Years   Breakthrough Years   Leadership Years

■ Knowledge   ▨ Behaviour   ■ Network

Being specific, you'll struggle to get on if you can't work constructively with your colleagues and clients. Even if you see yourself as, say, a technology wizard, you still need to engage with the people you meet and build productive relationships. That's an integral part of their 'experience' of you and hence an integral part of your performance in your role. If people can't or don't want to work with you, your contribution is devalued as you become difficult to engage with.

In summary, as we progress through our working lives, there are three elements that determine the impact we can make.

A. Our Knowledge – the things we are paid to be able to do
B. Our Behaviour – the way we engage with people and build relationships
C. Our Network – the range of people who know and remember us positively

The best tactic for improving your 'luck' and building your active support network is to:

- Stay competent and informed on A

- Engage in meaningful conversations at every opportunity on B

- Stay in touch helpfully with the people you meet on C

It's that simple.

5. Building Your Brand Through Conversations

We said early in this book that you can get lucky in your career by having good conversations. We have also said that relationships are built one interaction at a time and that it is critical to make the most of every interaction. Let's now look at a variety of interactions and conversation types that together can really build your brand and get you known, trusted, understood and valued.

We will look at seven types of interaction that have a significant impact on the development of your Business Brand:

- Your online business image – how you talk to the world

- Formal presentations – talking to people after a presentation

- Your behaviour in unstructured group situations – how you should spend your time when there are many people you could talk to

- Your behaviour in one-to-one planned meetings – making the most of this precious opportunity

- Your behaviour in planned meetings with more than two attendees – being joined up and making a contribution

- Your behaviour when a conversation opportunity happens unexpectedly – making it about them, not you

- Your preparation for an interview – making it a two-way conversation.

and learn how to be memorable and useful.

We'll start with your online presence.

Talking to the World

Your online business image

What do people do if they know they are going to meet you? In the business world, they are likely to Google you and the first thing they expect to come up is your LinkedIn profile. If you don't have a LinkedIn profile, you are missing out on being easy to find and having an easy way to stay in touch with the connections you make over time.

Your LinkedIn profile is effectively your personal website. It is not your CV, though many people do treat it as if it is and only pay it any attention when they are looking for a new job. That's really under-using and under-valuing what a good profile page can do for you.

From your first days in a work environment, make sure you do these six things:

1. Sign up for LinkedIn

2. Add a suitably professional-looking photo. Look business-like

3. Customise your LinkedIn address to be your own name

4. Have a headline statement that sets the right expectation about you

5. Write a helpful summary

6. Add any professional qualifications

Let's look at these in a bit more detail.

1. Sign Up

   Go to www.linkedin.com and get started.

2. Your Photo

   My rules are simple.

✓ You must have one. A missing photo looks like you have something to hide. That's not a good message to be sending.

✓ Make sure it actually looks like you so people will recognise you in the flesh.

✓ Don't crop a holiday or night-out photo.

✓ Use a photo that portrays the image you want to project. It will be different in the creative industries to the legal profession. Choose carefully.

✓ Don't have a distracting background unless it is directly relevant to your business.

3. Edit Your LinkedIn Profile URL

   Once you have created your account, click to Edit Your Public Profile. You will then have an option to Edit Your Public Profile URL. Change it to be something recognisable and memorable. This helps you and search engines.

   Mine is www.linkedin.com/in/carolegillespie

4. Strong Headline Statement

   If you do nothing, LinkedIn will fill this in with your most recent job title and company name. e.g. Graduate Trainee at Tech Company X. You can leave the default or make it more interesting and informative. This becomes increasingly important as your experience increases over time, but why not start as you mean to go on.

   Here are a couple of examples:

- Economics Graduate | Student Accountant | Amnesty Advocate or

- Technology Apprentice | Team Representative | Linguist

It is all a question of the first impression you want to create.

As your career progresses, your headline statement can evolve with you.

For example:

Cyber-Security Specialist | Practice Leader | Industry Speaker

The alternative style is to make a statement about what you enable people to achieve. This is particularly useful for young entrepreneurs. For example:

Making Customers Sticky or Bringing Science to Life in Primary Schools.

Choose what's right for you. Just choose carefully and consider the impression you want to make. Role titles in your headlines statement rarely make an impression. Their place is in the Experiences section of your profile.

These first four are easy to do, so do them now.

5. Summary Statement

Many people waste this section. Some don't bother to complete it. Some just give a summary of what their business does. Some give a CV summary. This is your opportunity to 'talk' to anyone who reads your profile; to enable them to start to feel they know you. What you want when someone reads your profile summary is for them to feel that the two of you are 'on the same page' and that they can sense your personality. Other than that, there are no rules. Be different.

Write it in the first person and make sure that the first two lines say something interesting as only these show automatically. People have to click to read the rest.

e.g.1   Choosing between a degree and an apprenticeship scheme was difficult. In the end I chose the apprenticeship route. Here's why.
… I'm now two years into my apprenticeship, so did I make the right decision?…

Taking this type of approach to your summary statement is very different to writing a CV summary. If you take the trouble to share something you feel will be interesting and authentic, you will communicate part of your personality and hopefully engage with any readers. Don't go overboard with the number of words. Make it a useful exercise in capturing only the most important and helpful aspects.

e.g.2   I've always been fascinated by the power of music to enhance people's lives. Link music, technology and psychology and one creates a real force for transformation. In many countries around the world, obesity is a huge issue which costs lives and absorbs resources. My goal is to bring the power of the former to tackle the latter – and that's what I have now done with my new Tone Down app. This means rapid and sustainable weight loss accessible to everyone. Please try it and let me have your feedback.

Yes, this is about the person's business, but it talks from the point of view of the reader (their context not yours). It is helpful and informative and also communicates enthusiasm.

e.g. 3   As a student, my work and life experiences come from my holiday jobs and my travels. Here are the top three things I've learnt the hard way and which I intend to apply when I start my first real job.

1.
2
3.

Many people say they have nothing worth writing about when they are at or near the start of their careers. Everyone has something. Share what others might value such as the example above.

6. Special Things

If you've made the effort to gain a qualification or volunteer, then list it.

There are several sections. Help people to see the breadth of your capability and your passions. On their own, they won't change your fortunes, but they might help someone feel you have a shared interest or expertise.

In Summary

Make the most of being on LinkedIn and don't let your other online presences let you down.

> *Relationship Reminder:*
> *What goes online, stays online.*

The beauty of being on LinkedIn is that when you meet people, it is easy for the two of you to connect. You will then be advised when something changes for the people you are connected with, e.g. they change jobs, they are in the news, they have a birthday, they publish an article or post something. Any of these gives you the opportunity to get in contact with them to acknowledge the change or achievement in their life. They will appreciate that and you will be able to stay in touch very efficiently.

Talking After Formal Presentations

Conversations outside of the presentation

Suppose you are giving a presentation. That might be to two or three people or it might be to 200–300 people. There is a lot of advice on creating and giving good presentations and we won't cover that here.

However, most of the time, the main benefit from giving a presentation is the conversations that are had *after* the presentation takes place.

Many presenters stay in 'emit' mode instead of going into 'understanding' mode. If you've given a presentation, the big personal opportunities are the connections and feedback you get afterwards. Instead of continuing to try to show how clever and knowledgeable you are (you should already have established your credibility via your presentation), try asking questions like:

"What did you get from the presentation? How will that affect what you do next?"

"What was the most surprising thing that came out of the session for you?"

"What might you change as a result of the presentation?"

"How has the session helped your thinking?"

In those after-presentation sessions, the focus has to switch from you to the individual listener. If you continue to do the talking, you will miss the opportunity to understand the scale of impact you have had on each person in the audience. It only takes one person for whom it has a profound impact to make the effort worthwhile for both of you. Make sure you find out who that is.

***

Q&A15: Speaking at a seminar

I've been asked to speak at a seminar and I don't know whether to say yes or no. I'm not an extrovert and it feels like it would be a lot of effort for not much reward, especially as it will be at a time when I am very busy. However, I am working in an area where we are doing some really exciting work and it would be nice to share some of the thinking and maybe get some feedback on what other people are doing. So do I keep my head down and spend the time on making progress on my project, or bite the bullet and do my first seminar? How do I decide?

Aisha

Aisha,

Firstly, you don't need to be an extrovert to speak at a seminar. You just need to know your stuff and be willing to put the effort in to make it interesting and understandable to your audience. Whether you are speaking to a small internal gathering or substantial external group, it makes very little difference. For the purposes of answering your question, let's assume that you have enough time between now and the seminar to be able to do a good job of standing up and speaking. Prepare well in advance and rehearse with a person who will give you constructive feedback and you should do well. So should you do it?

It is fairly easy to work out what you have to put in – the time beforehand to write and rehearse, the time on the day, plus any travel time. But what can you get out of it. If we know that, we can see if the equation balances for you.

Here are three things to get you going on working out if this seminar is right for you:

1. *It will make you think about how to communicate what you are working on in terms that anyone can understand. We so often get wrapped up in doing things, we forget to step back and ask ourselves the "so what?" questions – i.e. Why does what you are working on matter? What impact has it/can it have? What relevance does it have to your audience/others? Getting this clear in your own mind and finding a way to express this clearly and simply will make your work more meaningful when you are asked about it outside the seminar setting. This is always worth doing. Preparing for a seminar is one way of forcing yourself to think this through.*

2. *Being a speaker enhances the number of people who are aware of you, your expertise and style. Question: is this an audience you want to reach?*

3. *One of the big benefits of being a speaker, and hence a person of authority on your subject, is that people will seek you out for a conversation. Question: What opportunity is there to spend time with members of the audience outside the presentation? What would you want to get out of an opportunity for informal conversation afterwards?*

There may well be other things that matter to you in making your decision, but these three are a good basis. If it is an audience you want to reach, who will get value from what you say and who you can have conversations with afterwards that should be helpful to you and them ... then go for it and prepare properly so everyone gets value from the session.

***

Talking in Unstructured Groups

Mixing and talking in networking environments

We all end up from time to time in a room with people we don't know. If we don't speak to people, we are missing a golden opportunity to get to know others in our company/industry/profession. How you go about the beginning, the middle and the end of those conversations is what will determine how pleasant and useful they are to you and the other person.

Before we go any further let me comment on Networking Events.

These are events that people choose to go to in the hope that they will make helpful contacts. Many organisations encourage their staff to get out in the marketplace and be seen at these things. Some even encourage their staff to go and to hand out and collect business cards.

Given our busy lives and the limited likelihood of a random meeting at one of these events producing a meaningful outcome, I choose not to go unless one or both of the following are true:

1. There is something about the event that is really interesting to me and/or highly relevant to my business, e.g. a great speaker or a topic being covered that I am really interested in.

2. There is at least one person at the event that I specifically want to speak to because there is potentially something of value to each of us to discuss. Ideally, there would be three or four people.

If you can't tick at least one of these boxes, don't waste your time. Relax at home, spend time with your partner, go to the gym, read a book. If you are going to make the investment of going, then do it properly. To help you do this, always ask for the guest list beforehand. It won't often be available, but it is invaluable to your preparation when it is.

So, whether the opportunity to mingle comes from your own choice, via a company gathering or simply a gathering in a room before a meeting, make the most of it.

***

Q&A16: Networking effectively

I am going on my first cross-organisation training course next week. I currently work in a small team in the North and I will be joining up with people from around the world. I'm both excited at the prospect of meeting so many new people and getting to understand how we all fit together, but also quite daunted by the idea of being in such a big group between our training sessions. I want to make the most of the training and the networking, but don't know how. I suspect I will either come over as timid or pushy. Neither would be good. How do I strike the right balance and really get to know my wider colleague group in a way that will show the real me?

Martin

Martin,

What a great opportunity for you. I expect there will be lots of times when you will be in small groups as well as large ones. In some of these smaller ones it will be easy to talk and there will be natural subjects such as the session that has just finished or about to start. In every session, try to remember the name of the person you are talking to.

When they introduce themselves, say their name back to them. So, instead of just saying "Hi, I'm Martin," concentrate on them and say "Hi Lisa, I'm Martin." Just saying the name helps it to stick. Do the same when you finish the conversation "Nice talking to you Lisa." More generally, if you can get a list of the attendees from the organisers you can see who is attending and mark off who you have met, along with any relevant info about them.

You will probably also have some larger gatherings such as a social session and dinner on your last night or even just coffee breaks between sessions when there are lots of your colleagues around. If I am in an environment like this where I don't know anyone, I try to think and act like a host. So I introduce myself to people who are on their own and looking uncomfortable and invite people to join a conversation group that I am in. This is a really nice way to be friendly and helpful. Then, be a good listener. Ask them a question to get the conversation going and then listen to what they say. Try to understand them and ask clarification questions to make sure you have understood.

A piece of advice I have found very useful is "Listen with a view to understanding, not with a view to responding."

It is so easy to miss something important that has been said, because we are busy formulating our next sentence. Let the person finish. Don't share your anecdote or comment until the person is ready to hear. That way you will learn a lot and come over well. When you are asked about yourself and your role in the organisation, have a couple of sentences on the end result of your work rather than the tasks you perform. That's what will interest people and make for an interesting conversation.

Lastly, smile. It is much easier to approach someone who is smiling than to approach someone with their head down and giving off 'stay away' vibes. Be welcoming to the people around you and you'll have no problem getting to know lots of new people in your organisation.

***

Talking in 1-1 Planned Meetings

Precious time with an individual

When you get time with an individual and it is just you and them, this is something quite special these days. So much is done by email and text, it can be quite a big decision to spend time in a face-to-face conversation. No matter what the primary purpose of the conversation (e.g. planned review, feedback session, priority setting, planning meeting), we should always strive to make progress at a personal level as well as on the main objective.

***

Q&A17: Making a meeting productive

I've a meeting in the diary next week. It's with my new People Manager. We've not met before and he's asked for a session for us to get to know each other and see what the future might hold. How do I make a really good

impression?

Angeli

Angeli,

Before we talk about this meeting specifically, let me give you a way to think about any one-to-one meeting. These face-to-face sessions are a real opportunity to make progress on all the Relationship Pillars, but only if you prepare properly. Even if you are not the leader/owner of the meeting, you will probably waste this opportunity if you simply 'turn up'.

Here's what you can do to enhance your reputation in a one-to-one meeting.

1. *Make sure there is clarity on what a meeting is trying to achieve, before you both turn up.*

   This is different to what a meeting is about. The meeting might be about 'how your project is going' or 'what additional training might be appropriate for you'. What the meeting might be trying to achieve is 'identification of the two or three things that would enable the project to deliver earlier' or 'agreement on what course would be most relevant this year and the best timing for it'. See the difference? The latter statements allow you to judge whether the meeting has been worthwhile.

   Knowing where you both need to get to is the fundamental basis for a productive meeting.

   In your specific situation, you've told me that your meeting is about 'getting to know each other' and to 'see what the future might hold'. How will you know you've achieved this? What result will make the meeting worthwhile for you and your People Manager? As a minimum be clear in your own mind on what these could/should be, e.g. I need to know how we are going to work together, what I should expect from him and vice versa, understand his background and what he found helpful at my stage in his career. Decide on the top three things that will give you a strong basis for getting value from the relationship. Do the same for 'What the future holds'. Is this about geography, role, salary, promotion, specialisms, training .... ? Again, decide what would be a good result from a conversation on 'What the future might hold'.

Just because this is what you would like as the outcome, doesn't mean your People Manager has the same picture. He may have no specific view, or might have a very specific intended outcome. It would be good to know before you go into the meeting and getting him to think about exactly what he wants is good too.

2. *Prepare for the meeting.*

Think about how you and the other person might reach the end result. If the People Manager sends you an agenda, review it and refine it if need be. It's only the two of you in the meeting, so make it work for both of you. Don't be shy in suggesting changes to the agenda or ways to make it more explicit. If you are not sent an agenda by a week before the session, send one of your own with a focus on the outcomes required.

The three things that are generally valuable to you and valued by the other party are:

- *Before the meeting: Making sure there is shared clarity on the purpose and outcome required from the meeting, and creation of a structure for the meeting that can make that happen.*

- *During the meeting: Be ready with good questions that will be helpful in fulfilling your objectives. Capture the agreements/decisions as they happen and play back at the end of the meeting.*

- *After the meeting: Summarise the important items agreed and deliver on the things you have committed to do.*

What you'll hopefully realise is that I am saying that you need to behave in the meeting as two equals talking to each other rather than a senior person talking to a junior person. Your preparation can enable you to do as much asking and understanding as the other person. That will make you stand out far more than someone who is passive and waits to be told what to do.

***

Talking in planned meetings with more than two attendees

Being joined-up and making a contribution.

The more people in a meeting, the more important it is that you know what the meeting is trying to achieve and what is expected of you. It never ceases to amaze me how many people go in to a meeting with no clear idea of how the meeting will be run, who will run it, what each person's role is and how the goal(s) of the meeting will be reached.

Worse still are meetings where there is no clarity on the goals. Without clear goals and a way to judge if they have been achieved, meetings are just a place for people to talk and usually achieve very little.

If you are attending a meeting, be it internal or external, you need to know a minimum of four things beforehand:

1. Who will be there?

2. What is the intended outcome of the meeting (i.e. what decision is to be taken)?

3. How does the leader of the meeting plan to reach the intended outcome?

4. What is your role in enabling the outcome to be achieved?

It can be such a wasted opportunity when the person leading a meeting has only a vague idea of either what a great outcome is or how to get to that outcome. If it is an external meeting, you might hear phrases like "To get to know the client better" or "To tell them about our services" or "To see how we can help them." These are much too general to give structure to a conversation. More disappointing still is that there is often little explicit and shared clarity on what will make a meeting valuable to each party. If these things are not known, it is most unlikely that a meeting that is worthwhile to all parties will occur. So, what can you do?

If you are asked to attend a meeting, start with the four questions above. Don't be afraid to ask the 'stupid' question of "How exactly will we judge that?" if you get a bland and generic answer to question two.

Similarly, "How will this approach get us to the intended outcome?" should force the meeting leader to be more specific. Lastly comes your role. You should now be in a position to establish what your contribution is in the meeting. If there is not a purpose to your attendance, there is no point in you being there.

**

Q&A18: Participation in a meeting

My Project Manager has suggested that I come to the review meeting next week with our client. She says this will be useful for my personal development. I think the Head of Finance and the Programme Manager from our client will be there, as well as the Relationship Manager and my Project Manager from our side. I won't have anything useful to say and I'm going to feel rather stupid just sitting there. How can I get out of going without offending my Project Manager who thinks she is doing me a favour?

Max

Max,

What a negative attitude to take. You are lucky enough to have someone trying to help you in your career and yet you are ready to turn your back on it because you might feel a bit uncomfortable.

People don't learn much when they stay in their comfort zone all the time. It's when we are doing something that takes us outside that zone that we grow and develop. Stop being so fearful and start making an effort to make the most of this opportunity.

1. *Speak with your Project Manager and ask her for 15 minutes to help you get prepared for the meeting.*

2. *Find out how she thinks being in the meeting will help your personal development. Is it visibility of part of the role of a Project Manager or an opportunity for you to meet the relationship manager or are they discussing part of the project directly related to your own work? Make sure you get a clear answer. Set aside a time after the meeting to assess what you did get from it.*

3. *Agree what you are going to do in the meeting and how you will be introduced so everyone is clear on why you are there, e.g. "This is Max from our team. He is joining us today as part of his personal development programme. He will be listening and capturing the main points of the meeting."*

4. *Even if all you are doing is capturing the main points, this is hard work. You'll have to listen very hard. Ask if there is anything you can to do before the meeting to be able to do your role well.*

5. *In the meeting, concentrate, listen and observe. Be ready to answer a question or two by your clients on what you have got out of the meeting. I would expect them to be interested in your view.*

6. *Have the debriefing session with your Project Manager. She is genuinely trying to help you so make sure you take the trouble to think through what you got from attending the meeting. There is always something, but what it is can be unpredictable.*

7. *Say thank you for the opportunity. That's polite and she deserves it.*

The only possible reason to consider trying to back out of an opportunity like this is if you have no way to do the basic preparation. Given your Project Manager is trying to help you, I think this is most unlikely.

Be grateful for the opportunity and do your bit by making a contribution in the meeting and giving honest and constructive feedback afterwards.

***

Talking Reactively

Handling ad hoc conversations

Often the hardest conversation to have is the one we are not expecting. It might be an introduction to a senior person before a meeting on a client site, or maybe an introduction to a person from a different department when you are having lunch in the canteen. Even if all they say is "Nice to meet you. What do you do?" or "What does your company do?" many people struggle to answer this appropriately. It ought to be so easy, but it's not, even for people well established in their careers. The most common mistake is to assume that the person has asked the question because they are interested in knowing the answer. Often they are just being polite and are expecting maybe a simple, one sentence answer. That doesn't mean you shouldn't have a good answer and a way to find out whether what you each do is relevant to the other.

***

Q&A19: Describing what you do

My boss has told me that I have to learn to give an 'Elevator Pitch' for our business. It feels horribly forced when I say it and I don't know what to do after I've said it. It's so uncomfortable for me and the other person and very embarrassing. I'd like to be able to deliver it well, but little help is at hand. How do I do this in a way that is comfortable and helpful?

Jack

Jack,

You don't say what your role is in your organisation. I am going to assume that you are not in sales, and that there is a desire by the management team for everyone to be able to contribute to finding new business opportunities. In that context it is reasonable that everyone should be able to answer the question "What does your business do?" and a so-called Elevator Pitch is one way that people try to make it easier to answer. The problem comes exactly as you describe it that you have not been told when to use it, how to use it and what to expect or do when you've used it. I absolutely understand why you feel uncomfortable.

Let's start by being clear on what an Elevator Pitch is supposed to be. One definition is that it is an informal term used to describe a brief speech that outlines the fundamental elements of a product, service, project or even a person. The name comes from the notion that the speech should be delivered in the time it takes for an elevator or lift ride, i.e. 20–60 seconds.

The idea behind a good Elevator Pitch is that in a very short amount of time you can make someone want to know more about you and/or your business, i.e. it is first and foremost a conversation starter, not an end in itself. This clearly has not been explained to you. Many people think it is about going into selling mode. When people who are not sales people try to use an Elevator Pitch they usually feel they are being asked to sell and that creates real discomfort. If we change your perspective, maybe you can get comfortable with what is really quite a helpful but often misused and misunderstood concept.

Your discomfort is not helped by the words 'Pitch' and 'Speech' that also give the wrong impression. Both these words probably create an expectation in your mind that this is something you have to learn by heart and then deliver at every opportunity. Typically Pitches and Speeches are where one person talks and another listens – one way traffic. If that happens, it is a real wasted opportunity. Here's an example of a comfortable and helpful conversation that includes something that could be considered to be a form of Elevator Pitch.

A: Hi I'm Carole from 'People Buy From People'.

B: That's an unusual name for a company. What do you do?

A: We enable businesses to achieve results through relationships and create a balanced, enduring and productive portfolio of clients. That means they win good business, more easily and more often and ultimately end up with a more valuable business.

Or maybe…

We enable professional services organisations to win business without selling by the way relationships are created and sustained. That means senior professionals who are not sales professionals can do good business, more easily, more often in a way that feels comfortable and clients like and value.

What about your business?

B: *We're accountants and I run the tax practice.*

Or maybe …

I sell luxury cars, mainly Porsche and top of the range BMWs.

A: *So you will be involved in bringing new business into your company. What's your approach to finding new clients and looking after them over the years? …*

The two things to take from this very short example are:

1. *These things sound much better when spoken than read. By all means write down a few ideas, but you must speak them out loud.*

2. *You can have more than one Elevator Pitch adapted to various audiences, ranging from your hairdresser to your mum to delegates at a seminar to the person you meet on holiday. Just make sure it answers two questions: What result do you enable people to achieve, and why does that matter?*

   Do check that the Elevator Pitch you've been given meets these two criteria.

When you have given your brief and helpful overview (as that is what it is), ask a question of the other person to get the conversation going properly. Ideally, it should be a question that helps each of you to understand each other better. I asked two questions above, to understand their business and to start to discuss how they find and care for clients. I'm NOT selling. I am trying to UNDERSTAND.

Your Elevator Pitch should enable you to ask questions that help you understand the person you are talking to and, as the conversation progresses, you will each be able to see if anything you do is relevant to the person you are speaking to. In most cases, it probably won't be. However, on occasions, a conversation started like this will end up with a natural agreement that a more detailed conversation is worthwhile. That's exactly how it should be.

This doesn't come easily, so go and find someone else in your organisation who feels equally uncomfortable and role play together. Practise introducing yourself, saying variations on your Elevator Pitch out loud and responding with follow up questions depending on the answers given. Oh, and by the way, also have one or two very short examples, e.g. "For example, one of my clients joined an international consulting business as a direct entry partner and took his first client from $10k billing to $6m billing in his first six months." An example is the best way to bring the overview to life.

So now you know it is about starting an interesting conversation and not about selling your company's services at every opportunity.

Explicitly, it is an opportunity to make it very easy to establish together whether what you do is relevant. If it isn't, you'll still have an interesting conversation, but not one that will lead to business. That's as equally valuable as one that does, as it stops you wasting business development time in a place where there is no potential for business. Sell. Sell. Sell. Not!

***

Unexpected or ad hoc sessions catch many people off guard.

The big message is "Start a conversation." Do that by asking the other person an open question.

> *Relationship Reminder:*
>
> *Seek to understand before you seek to be understood.*

Talking in an Interview

Making it a two-way conversation

If you go for an interview, you know when, where, and often who will interview you, so there should be no excuse for preparing poorly. The problem is that many people don't know how to prepare in a way that has the potential to enable them to really engage with the interviewer.

Many organisations have online pre-screening tests. If these are included in your selection process, take advantage of the opportunity to practise example tests in advance of the real thing.

However, when it comes to meeting a real person and having your interview, just think of it as having an interesting conversation. So, what makes a conversation interesting? Usually it is when both parties have a point of view, ask good questions, give thoughtful answers and try to understand where the other person is coming from. Essentially this means a reasonably equal amount of talking by both parties.

That might sound odd as most people expect the interviewer to be asking all the questions to find out about you, but think again. You need to understand what they are looking for so you will know why you might be right for the role and whether you even want to work with the organisation concerned. They typically want to understand what has motivated you to apply, what you think you might contribute and why they might choose you rather than one/some of the other candidates.

***

Q&A20: Getting ready for an interview

I have been asked to attend an interview for a place on an apprentice training scheme with an engineering company. I'm sure I'd be good as an engineer, as I love designing, building and repairing things.

However, I've never had any real experience of being interviewed. What will they ask me? What do I have to say to show I would be a great apprentice for them? This is my chance for a great future. I don't want to blow it.

Rakesh

Rakesh,

As with many things in life, you can't control what your interviewer is like or the questions that will be asked. All you can control is what you do and say. If you are serious about wanting this apprenticeship, and it sounds as if you are, then let's concentrate on how you can prepare.

Advance thinking about the questions you will ask and the questions you will be asked is key.

Get Prepared*: Research*

Understand the basics of the business: what it does, where it does it, its strengths, competitors, etc.

Understand the scheme you are applying for: how long, how many people, what do you learn, what happens at the end, etc.

These are the things is it reasonable for the interviewer to assume you know and understand. If you can't be bothered to find this out in our search-engine enabled world, you can't be very interested. Be able to summarise the main points if asked. Be clear and succinct.

Get Prepared*: Your Questions*

What do you want to ask about that is not available on the internet?

For example, how will you decide who to offer an apprenticeship to? What percentage of those who join, complete the scheme? Why do people drop out? What are recently qualified apprentices doing now? How will you judge progress on the scheme? What's the most important attribute that predicts success on the programme?

These types of questions show you have thought about the scheme. They will probably also make the interviewer think too. That's no bad thing. It makes the conversation that much more interesting.

Don't forget to ask, "What happens next?"

Get Prepared*: Your Point of View*

Research and question prep is essential. It enables you to demonstrate real interest, shows your desire to understand and fuels a conversation. To take things to the next level, it is good to have a view on things relevant to the business or the role, for example what's likely to be the next big thing in the engineering industry? Is it maybe AI or new materials or 3D printing? If you understand this, you can ask a good question about it and discuss its application in the business. It shows you are well informed and thinking more widely about the environment you are coming into.

Get Prepared: *Your Motivation*

It is likely you will be asked "Why this business/industry?" and "Why this scheme?" Do have an answer. Make use of the Relationship Code behaviour of 'Their Context Not Yours' as you think about your answer. Make sure it is clear how your choice aligns with what they are trying to do, for example – "I've thought hard about university versus an apprenticeship. In looking at your scheme it seems to have the technical rigour of a university course combined with much greater hands-on experience. I enjoy understanding the theoretical structure behind how things work, and then get a real kick when it comes to life in a functional item. Your programme has the right balance and your business focuses on large road and rail infrastructure projects. These are so critical to the success of the country and I'd be proud to make a real contribution in this area."

Please don't use superlatives such as I'm passionate about ... They always sound false and are hard to back up if challenged.

Get Prepared: *Describing Yourself*

It is not uncommon for an interviewer to kick off by asking "Tell me about yourself." They already have your CV so don't fall into the trap of regurgitating it. Plan for this question and try formulating an answer that helps them see that you would be a natural choice for the position. Just because someone asks a question, doesn't mean you can't ask a question back to refine your answer, e.g. "What would you like to know specifically?"

What you don't want is long rambling monologue. Something short and sweet that leads into a conversation is much better. For example, "From my CV, you will have seen that I'm from Manchester, I've worked hard and got good BTech grades and am now deciding on how to take my career forward. What I think I've discovered over the past few years is that I've a talent for designing, building and fixing things. For example, I worked in a computer repair centre for one summer and on a building site for another. I ended up with quite a lot of responsibility in both cases and enjoyed seeing the results of my work. I also enjoy reading about new advances in materials science. These experiences have helped crystallise my decision to apply for this engineering apprenticeship. That's me in a nutshell. What else would you like to know?" That's a helpful summary of you and your motivation and should lead to additional questions that will enable you to bring out your interests and experience.

If this all sounds like a lot of work, it is. But, if you want to have the best chance of standing out from the many other candidates, this is what you need to do. It will give you the confidence to make the interview a two-way dialogue where you get as much out of it as the interviewer and your personality can shine through. As I said at the start, you can't control who the interviewer is or what they ask. You can be ready to make sure the two of you have a very interesting conversation and they understand how much you will put in to making the apprenticeship a success if they choose you.

Get Practice

Now you've done the prep, use it in a safe environment. In the same way as you might study for an exam and then do past papers to make sure you can apply your knowledge, the same is true for interviews. Go find someone – teacher, family friend, buddy – who is willing to interview you for the role in question. Tell them a bit about the company and the apprenticeship scheme beforehand, then, do the interview totally in role from the moment you sit down to practise to the time you finish and say goodbye. At the end, get feedback from the person who is helping you. What felt good to them? When did you talk too much? What did you say that really engaged them? How might you express yourself better in some areas? Take all the feedback you can. Think about it, refine your preparation and do it again with the same or a different person. Each time you do it, it will be more natural and your communication should improve. You can also get used to asking questions of the interviewer as you go along.

You don't have to wait until they ask if you have any questions. Once you feel *well prepared both mentally and in using your prep out loud, you are ready for the real thing.*

Oh, and don't forget to look the part when you turn up – on time, clean, tidy and a smile please.

Good luck.

***

6. Keeping the Conversation Going

It's all very well having a really good first conversation, but as with all initial contact, if that one conversation is all you have, you'll quickly be forgotten. Equally, probably none of us have the time to be meeting up with our network constantly. That's just not practical. What do we do instead?

What are the ways to interact and stay in touch? Here are the main ones:

- Meet and speak face-to-face

- Speak on the phone

- Text

- Share information that is relevant to an individual

- Share information to multiple specific recipients

- Share information to multiple non-specific recipients

- Use social media

Let's divide these into two types:

1. Those that need the active agreement of the other person before the interaction can happen.

2. Those that are fully under your own control.

It is only really when your aim is to speak with a person at a specific time that explicit agreement is needed for it to take place. That's because this mode of interaction demands a time commitment from the other person, not to mention one from you as well. Face-to-face meetings and most phone calls need to be about something that justifies the time both of you will devote to making it happen and to the meeting or conversation itself.

If you meet someone and then keep asking to meet up or talk when there is no reason to do so, you will quickly become an annoyance. What you do need to do is stay remembered so that when it is relevant to talk, it feels a natural and useful thing to do.

Under Your Own Control

For most people, staying in touch with friends and family via social media is an integral part of each day. Whether it is WhatsApp or Snapchat or your own favourite app, this just happens naturally. Your messages and pictures don't feel like an intrusion. What we also learn from these digital communications is that people respond in different ways. Or, more precisely, only some will respond. Not everyone will click the 'like' button when you post a picture on Instagram. That doesn't mean they haven't seen it or that they don't like it. It just means they haven't reacted to it digitally. You might like everyone to like your blog, but that doesn't happen.

The same is true for staying in touch with people in your business network. If you share an interesting article with your LinkedIn contacts, you won't expect everyone to like it or comment. They will register who sent it and have a view on its value to them, and that reinforces your Known and Valued Relationship Pillars. It's just that you won't have explicit feedback from them. Be prepared for the level of feedback to be a lot less than on your personal social media sites.

Relationship Reminder:

To be remembered, be helpfully visible.

***

Q&A21: Staying connected

I've been employed for about three years and in that time I've met quite a few people via the work I've been doing for them. One thing I've been very good at (I think) is keeping a note of who I've met plus their contact details etc. It used to be easy to stay connected with these people, e.g. by an occasional coffee or chatting during our lunch break or by a conversation when we were attending the same meetings. I'm now finding that people are moving onwards, upwards and outwards, as am I, and it is hard to keep track of everyone I already know. How on earth do I manage to do this as the numbers of contacts get bigger and more widespread?

Meimei

Meimei,

Good for you for making the conscious effort to stay connected and visible with the people you have met so far. You've made a fantastic investment into your Relationship Bank Account that has the potential to blossom over the coming years.

You ask an excellent question. As the numbers of people in your network increases, how do you stay remembered, and remembered for the right reasons?

Let's look at this from two perspectives: 1. How strong do you want your Relationship Pillars to be? 2. How do you make that happen, without it taking hours every day?

To have a Being Known Pillar, you have to be visible. This is the minimum requirement for a business relationship to exist. Whether you have ten people in your network or 10,000 you need to stay visible. If you make a point of being connected to the people you know via LinkedIn you have a simple way to jog their memory that you exist. Just share, comment or like an interesting article/quotation/infogram etc.

It's like your personal social media activity but in a business context. The only difference is that you will be making public things that can enhance your Business

Brand rather than your Personal Brand on a business rather than personal topic. Someone who shares every day may get blocked. People can't handle huge volumes of this type of communication, so be selective. An average of once every two to four weeks is fine for this type of general sharing of useful/interesting material. If you choose well, you will also nudge along your Being Valued Pillar.

Now let's think about whether there are things you can do that explicitly enhance your Business Brand by adding even more value to the recipients. Here's a question for you. You don't say what industry you are working in, so over the next five years, what do you want to be famous for? Is it as a 'shake up the establishment entrepreneur', a 'lawyer for the disadvantaged', a 'digital creative talent', a 'quirky travel writer'? If you know how you want to be perceived, start sharing and commenting on things in this space. You may still be relatively early in your career, but that doesn't mean you don't have a useful and different view. Better still, post your own views. Just make sure that your readers will get value from what you say to increase your Valued Pillar still further.

The above is still about staying visible and helpful with everyone in your network. You also need to be more specific for an individual when the opportunity arises. You say you have been keeping a note of the people you have met. Send them a message when something relevant changes, e.g. new job/location/promotion, they win an award, they are shortlisted for something, going on maternity leave or coming back, a work anniversary, they publish a book or send an article explicitly relevant to them … it could be anything. Make your note to them friendly and sincere. People usually appreciate this and respond to a personal note. I know I do. Again, LinkedIn helps you see what changes are happening in your network.

In summary, the more relevant your communication is to the person receiving it, the greater the impact on the Relationship Pillars of Being Known and Being Valued.

None of this takes much time or extra effort. Yes, you have to keep an eye open for things you can share. The added benefit is that this process is all part of what you should be doing anyway to continually keep yourself informed on what is going on in your industry and business area. You get a double whammy of staying in touch and keeping yourself informed. That's a really good investment on your part.

There is a time and place for coffee catch-ups, shared lunches etc.; just pace yourself as your network grows. You'll be surprised how easy it is to get back in touch with someone when the time is right, if you have been making the effort to stay helpfully visible.

***

My business is all about achieving results through relationships. I have met a huge number of people over the years. Am I still in touch with all of them? I can't claim that I am. That's partly because it is only relatively recently that this has become possible and because I only learnt later on how important and enjoyable it is be able to interact so easily with a diverse group of people. What I do do is write and share things with this group with the objective of giving people a different/useful way to think about business relationships and potentially change their behaviour and enhance their own success.

Hopefully that reinforces my reputation as a business relationships expert and makes a difference for at least some of my audience. I'm proud to be able to do this.

7. Protect and Enhance Your Brand

We've talked in this book about how our interactions create our Business Brand. In this chapter, we are going to consider the things beyond the way we interact that can add or detract from the impression we create.

At times we have talked not only about creating the right impression by our conversations, but avoiding creating the wrong impression. It is daft to put in the effort in one area for our impact to be undermined by things in other areas that are so easily under our own control.

Look the Part

Be conscious of what you are wearing says about you and especially the first impressions you create.

***

Q&A22: Dressing for success

I like to think that the way I dress gives off a cool and funky vibe. My clothes reflect my personality. They are always clean, original and well made (by me), but my manager told me that I should think about 'smartening up'. I was really offended at this. My work is very good and I always deliver, so why are they trying to interfere with what I'm wearing? Even if they don't like my outfits, surely they are not stupid enough to think it affects my work. I'm definitely not changing what I wear. How do I get my manager to accept that this is me, and that she should be looking at what I deliver, not my clothes?

Fatima

Fatima,

This has really touched a raw nerve. From what you say, it is clear that expressing yourself through your clothes is really important to you. I suspect you feel that you are being asked be a 'fake' you at work. I know that if I am uncomfortable, in all senses of the word, with what I am wearing, I struggle to do my best work. Let's think about your manager's motivation for asking you to 'smarten up'.

Firstly, did you ask her why she said this? I can think of a few reasons for what she said, and most are much more constructive than perhaps you give her credit for.

OK, maybe she is just narrow-minded and thinks everyone should 'conform' and adhere to a boring way of dressing at work. I'll start by assuming this is not the case.

More likely, it is because she really values your work and contribution, but has learnt over time that many people jump to conclusions about someone's abilities purely based on how they are dressed. That's sad but true. Our lazy brains are always jumping to conclusions. What she may be trying to do is to make it easier for your talents to be recognised more widely.

Or possibly, in a similar vein, there is the potential for you to be working directly with end-clients. You then represent not only yourself, but also your organisation. Your personal brand and your organisation's brand shouldn't be fighting each other. If they do, the clients you meet will find it harder to engage with you than you and your manager would like. Why put those barriers in the way?

I'm not going to tell you what to wear. It may be that you are a square peg in a round hole and you would be much happier in an environment where your style is more the norm. However, if you do like where you are working and want to stay, then some give and take is needed if you want it to be easy to be taken seriously. Try this to help you keep your individuality and still dress in a way that avoids the assumptions that can hold you back.

Take a look at the people who are the level above your manager. How are they dressing? Most of these will have a style that communicates professionalism, authority and competence. Pick a style that reflects how you want to be perceived. It might be as simple as wearing a smart jacket or avoiding mini-skirts. Take the style you see and adapt to your own, e.g. If most people at that level wear mainly black, keep your outfits colourful but similarly styled. There will be plenty of options.

Work out how you are going to adapt your style, put it into action and go back to your manager to ask advice on how you are doing. If you didn't ask before, ask now, what was the motivation for suggesting you change. You may find you have a real supporter who is genuinely trying to help you get on.

In terms of being yourself, there is nothing wrong with having a work style and a play style. In your own time, you can wear what you want. Be as extreme as you wish. Experiment to your heart's content. In the work environment, it makes sense to make it easy for people to relate to you. Making your clothes a barrier just doesn't make sense.

***

Much to my surprise, some years ago one of my clients commented on my clothes and asked for a change. The company I worked for and most of my clients were fairly formal so I mainly wore a skirt and jacket each day. However, I started working with one client where the standard form of dress was jeans and t-shirt, with 'dress down Friday' often flip flops and a definite distressed and skimpy look to the clothes. The MD took me aside and said "Carole, when are we going to get you in jeans?" He had realised that the formality of my dress made it harder for people to relate to me. I had thought that just taking my jacket off when I arrived was enough. It wasn't. Changing the way I dressed at that client did make a difference. It was a good challenge that I appreciated when I saw how it changed the way people responded to me and accepted me as an integral part of the team.

The approach I adopted was to wear jeans, add boots, but keep the jacket. I also wore my hair loose rather than tied up. That way I still felt smart and professional, but I was clearly part of the company vibe. I didn't go native, but I did fit in.

Look After Yourself

We've talked about how you dress, but what about the whole you? If you want to do well, you need the health to perform at your best. If you are all or any of sleep deprived, poorly nourished, generally unfit or under/overweight it will reflect in your ability to be the best you can. If you do nothing else, do these simple things to enhance your overall health and hence your ability to participate positively and enjoy the time you spend both inside and outside work.

Sleep – switch your electronic screens off after 9 pm. Hard I know. I don't always manage this. However, the blue light from these devices messes with our brainwaves and makes it much harder to fall and stay asleep. Try to settle at roughly the same time each night and get up at around the same time each morning. If you need to catch up on sleep during the working day, find a quiet corner during your break and set your alarm to wake you up after 20 minutes. That way you will get the benefit of a brain boost without it compromising your night time sleep (or your boss thinking you are skiving).

Food – By this I don't mean go on a diet. Your diet is simply what you eat. The word has been hijacked by the dieting industry to mean all sorts of weird ways of eating. Eating well is easy. Eat meat, fish, nuts, pulses, green vegetables and fruit … most of the time. Don't make cakes, crisps, bread, pasta, pastry, fizzy drinks and other carbohydrate and sugar rich foods a regular part of your diet. No one eats perfectly all the time; that's just not human nature. However, the degree to which your body is in balance is determined by what you eat most of, most of the time.

Some people call this having a primal diet (like our cave-dwelling ancestors) or more technically a low GI (glycaemic index) diet.

Essentially this way of eating lets you eat as much as you want to of foods that keep your insulin production in balance and hence stabilises energy and avoids hunger.

Drink – I've only one big MUST DO on this topic. Drink lots of water. Make your own choices about tea, coffee, sports drinks, energy drinks, alcohol, etc. Ideally drink in moderation most of the time. Aim to have a glass of water between each one of the above that you consume. You will feels so much better for it and your body will thank you with clearer skin and brighter eyes, better digestion and a happy liver among other things. During the day, keep water next to you. Make it really easy to drink it regularly by having it always to hand. Incidentally, the opposite applies to drinks or foods you are trying to avoid. Keep them out of sight and needing an effort to get them. I'm not sure of the exact statistics, but in an office, when 'perk' sweets were put in a jar with a top on, instead of being open, I believe consumption fell by about 80%.

In terms of both food and drink, the motto in my household is "Shopping is the first line of defence." If you don't buy it, you can't consume it. That's the ultimate in making it easy to eat well, by simply not having rubbish around. Also, don't go shopping when you are hungry as that's a sure-fire way to succumb to a sugar-laden treat.

Keep Moving – I'm not talking about moving to a new job. I am talking about keeping your body moving. We humans are not designed for sitting down.

Various studies have shown that sitting is really bad for our health. Some people love the gym. Others hate it, or simply can't afford it. The answer is to walk more. Whether it is stairs instead of lifts, feet instead of tubes or buses, a walk outside at lunchtime, even walking to the end of the road to post an old fashioned letter – keep moving. Everyone can manage 30 minutes of movement a day. Try to make it fast enough that you get slightly warm and slightly out of breath.

Even if you are working in an office, set your alarm to remind you to move at least once an hour. Better still, make that your cue to walk to the kitchen to get a glass of water. If you can make this a habit, the chances are you will have less ill health over the years. After all, you need to look after your body as it is the only place you have to live.

With these four tips for looking after yourself holistically, you are now really looking the part and have the energy, vitality and good health to perform well.

Next let's think about three things that boost your brand and make others feel good by your behaviour.

Time Management

In business, there is no such thing as being fashionably late. If you are supposed to be somewhere ready to work, be there. Turning up late is disrespectful and sends a message that you can't organise yourself and even that you are unreliable. Once, is forgivable if you have a good reason *and* you have let the meeting leader know you will be late. Otherwise, get organised and set an example for others to follow.

Meeting Behaviour

If you are in a meeting, be fully present. Hard though it is, switch your various devices off and put them away. You may think you can multi-task and check your emails as well as listen attentively to a presentation or a discussion, but you can't. Our brains don't work that way. Yes, you'll get the gist, but whoever is speaking deserves your full attention … because that is what you would want if the roles were reversed. Imagine you had spent time putting together a presentation to help your colleagues and then no one was listening to you. In this as all things, do as you would be done by.

> *Relationship Reminder:*
>
> *Put technology away and really concentrate on a conversation. You'll show and build respect and it's amazing what you will learn when you really listen.*

Body Language

Body language needs a book in its own right. I have just one golden rule on body language for you, and that is to smile. A smile when you meet people conveys your enthusiasm to meet them. A smile when you leave conveys the value of the conversation. Even a smile when you are talking to someone on the phone translates into your tone of voice and is perceived at the other end.

The weird thing about smiling is that of course we smile when we are happy, but it has also been shown that we feel happy when we smile. Our brain seems to recognise that we are smiling and releases the 'happiness' hormone into our bloodstream. This way you can make other people feel good and boost your own feeling of happiness too.

Lastly, learning is a lifelong activity. Stop learning and you will quickly become stale and irrelevant.

Stay Informed

We all need to be good at what we do. Many employers help us do this either through courses or on the job training. While we might be well versed in our own area of expertise, we could become rather boring if that is all we can talk about and have a point of view on. Going back to before the Millennium, how did people generally extend their wider knowledge? It was mainly through books, monthly (business) magazines, TV documentaries, etc. Today there are so many ways to delve into subjects of interest. How would we survive without our always available search engines? We use them all the time to check facts and answer questions. We can also use the same mechanism to widen our insight and experience a variety of perspectives on almost any topic.

Personally, I find it hard to read whole books other than on holiday. Then I love them and usually have a fiction and a non-fiction one on the go at the same time. However, when the working week is full-on, I enjoy reading short articles over a cup of coffee. Quite often I pick a topic, put it in my search engine and see what comes up.

As part of my writing for People Buy From People, I pick a different business relationships theme each month and produce a short article. In parallel with this, I try to find one or two really good short articles on the same general topic, but from a very different angle. Recently I wrote one on the topic of 'Shared Expectations'; how to make sure you are in explicit agreement and how a mismatch in expectations can lead to disappointment and worse. The most interesting complementary article I found was called 'Oh No! The Psychology of Disappointment'. In fact it was an infogram, which is a great way to communicate difficult topics very simply. I was then able to include these two articles in my monthly email for my followers. We all benefited.

The point to all this is that it is really easy to continually expose yourself to new ideas in and around your fields of interest and beyond. This broadens your own horizons, gives you interesting things to talk about and gives you things that you can use to help other people, by sharing with them.

A very old-fashioned phrase about self-development is to 'sharpen the saw'. If the saw is sharp it does a better job in much less time and with less effort.

Say no more.

Bringing Your Brand Together

This chapter has looked at how we can protect and further enhance our Business Brand. If we look the part, have the health and strength to perform well, our behaviour embraces the 'do as you would be done by' philosophy and we widen our perspectives, we will be all set to make a real impact within our organisation and beyond.

Thinking in this way is taking a 'bottom up' approach to our life and career. To bring this all together, let's stand back and take a 'top down' view.

People don't think about us in discrete parts, they perceive us as a whole. That means that if we don't know how we want to be perceived at work or at play, how can we consciously set about being that person?

In the workplace, you might want to be perceived as anything from having real gravitas to being a tough cookie to the person who always helps a person in need to being the quirky creative. We need to have thought about this so we can make choices about what we do and how we do it and take control of our overall Business Brand. It doesn't have to be complicated. It does have to be conscious.

Here are three questions for you:

- What are the five most common words that you believe people would use to describe you?

- What are the five words you would most like people to use about you now?

- What are the five words you'd like people to say about you when you are no longer around?

You can do this for your work persona and then for your play persona. Whilst there is some overlap, there are usually some differences too.

You might want to take a small sample from people in your network on the first question. The results are likely to be a bit biased as people like to be nice, but they might surprise you anyway by what they say. Don't be defensive if you disagree. Just ask questions to make sure you understand why they chose the words they did. Use this an input to answer the next question.

Let me bring this to life and share the five words that I would like people to use when they think and talk about me to encapsulate my Business Brand goal.

Here they are:

Enthusiasm. Focus. Fairness. Impact. Insight.

Here's my rationale:

Enthusiasm: If I'm not enthusiastic about what I'm doing, why should anyone else be? Enthusiasm is infectious. It gives other people the confidence to do things and makes any task more enjoyable.

Focus: Without clear priorities, we can say "yes" too often and try to do too much. "Yes" can be the easy option in the short term. The constructive use of "no" allows us to have more impact and achieve more of the things that are important. It avoids setting expectations that are likely to be unfulfilled. Unfulfilled expectations undermine relationships.

Fairness: This is about always being able to look someone in the eye and be proud of the way I've behaved. Ultimately, this is the foundation of any meaningful relationship. It also gives one the right to expect the same treatment in return.

Impact: It's easy to get wrapped up in the tasks that fill our days. There are times when I have found myself being pointlessly busy. Ultimately we will be judged by what we achieve, or enable others to achieve.

By concentrating on the outcomes that will bring about meaningful change or success I try to have a lasting impact.

Insight: This is about distilling, and then sharing, what I've learnt in a way that enables others to grow. That's the motivation behind this book.

As Nelson Mandela said, "Each one, teach one." That's the way to create a real legacy and truly multiply one's impact.

What could this add up to? Hopefully, it is someone who does what she says she will in a way that feels right, and enables others to have the confidence and capability to succeed in tackling important challenges. That is something I'd be proud to be known for. I hope this book will make a small contribution to you achieving your goals.

At the end of the day, you are what you do.

In business, an organisation's culture is the manifestation of the behaviour of the people in that company. Likewise the brand that people perceive is the result of our behaviour. At its core is our personal code of conduct and is the foundation for how we lead by example: consciously or otherwise.

As you are reading this book, it is a good bet that you are keen to have a brand you can be proud of, in both your business and personal life. If you are clear on the five words that define the Business Brand and the Personal Brand you aspire to, you will have a simple yet effective way to judge whether your intended actions will take you towards or away from that brand.

8. What Next?

Let's roll the clock forward, say, ten years. It sounds a long time, but like most things in life, it will pass in a flash. I'm not going to ask you where you see yourself or what you'll be doing then. Very few people can be explicit about this and often make something up if asked. The question is too specific. What you should be able to say is what you are setting out to achieve in this timeframe. Much of what we've talked about in this book is about focusing on outcomes rather than tasks during conversations. The same applies to your working life.

A good way to start thinking about this is to ask yourself "How will I decide if I am getting the most from my working life?" It then comes down to what success and fulfilment means to you.

Coming originally from a background where there was no guidance on navigating the world of work, my career has been a bit of a random walk. The individual things that have been important to me have varied as my circumstances have changed. At times flexibility and location have been a priority. At others it has been financial reward.

However, there have been four constants:

Continual learning: I need to be doing something where I am continuing to learn. I've left excellent organisations simply because I felt I was stagnating, and couldn't see a way out – other than to leave.

People I respect: If one always has to second-guess the motivations, commitment or capability of the people you work with, or the leaders of your organisation, it will undermine your own confidence. Conversely, it is amazing to work with and for people you trust and respect.

Constructive feedback: We all need feedback. Without it, it is difficult to understand our impact and how to develop further. Working in a vacuum is not for me. If one's work is good, recognition is a great motivator to continue the good work. If we are not making the grade, how can we learn and improve if we don't know what's not working?

Meaningful work: To know that what we are doing matters and is having a tangible outcome can be exhilarating. I find that being able to use one's talents in a positive way is highly energising.

What gives fulfilment to one's working life is highly personal. Any time spent in the world of work helps you to understand yourself and find your own constants. My own holiday jobs in a shoe shop and in a hearing-aid manufacturing company (among many), helped me to start to crystallise what both good and bad style jobs looked like for me. It also gave me the clarity and motivation to try to avoid the type of jobs that had characteristics that didn't suit me.

Even if we plot a career course, life has a habit of intervening. To help you navigate this and be open to options, take some time to think about how you will judge whether you are in an environment that suits you. Ignore the actual job elements; think instead about what will make it fulfilling for you. Then add in the specific current requirements. That will give you a great foundation for judging both.

I am often asked for career advice, e.g. "Should I stay or should I move?" "Should I choose this option or that option?" "How can I make my current situation better?"

Often it is not the specifics of a role that makes it attractive or unattractive. In fact, focusing on job specifics can make it hard to compare opportunities. However, if you compare two or more options in terms of how well they match your current and constant priorities, you'll have a way to filter what's right or wrong for you. Usually this makes a decision much easier, even if only by reducing the number of options you are looking at and giving you a way to discuss with others.

I've worked for multiple organisations and now have my own business. People often assume that I am very ambitious, but this is not strictly the case. Yes, I've wanted to do well, but the changes I've made over the years have been more about taking advantage of opportunities that fitted my priorities rather than a move to 'climb a ladder'. Maybe I'm lucky, but the moves I made did allow me to progress and do well.

Maybe that's because most of the time the roles fitted both my needs and the needs of the organisations I worked for. Did I understand this at the time? Definitely not. It took me many years to understand what was driving my decisions and why some were good and some less so. It is the same with building and sustaining contacts and relationships. I only worked out what this was all about quite a way into my career.

That's the ultimate rationale for this book – to give you the chance to set yourself up for success much more consciously than I was ever able to do. If you know what you are trying to achieve, and consciously and consistently set out to build the support network and visibility that can be helpful, you'll be able to navigate your career much more explicitly than I did. I hope this book will give you a way to be more in control of your life and create your own opportunities.

Wherever you come from, whatever your background, gender, orientation or colour of your skin, please remember:

"Discrimination is overcome one relationship at a time."

So go out there and build those relationships, and you will find people who will be ready to take a chance on you.

At the start of this book, we heard about Donald Rumsfeld's "unknown unknowns, known unknowns and known knowns." As someone new to the world of business, I didn't know that visibility and relationships were important, nor would I have known how to achieve this even if I'd been aware. I wasn't conscious of the brand I wanted to convey, other than one of energy and 'can do' mentality. I only had an inkling from my holiday jobs of what I didn't want to do (repetitive work with the same people every day, in the same place). I started with a lot of unknown unknowns. It's only more recently that I've been able to have real clarity on the things we've talked about in this book – networks, relationships, brand and priorities.

Give this some thought now. Your brand and priorities will change over time, but start to get to know yourself now so you have a basis for decisions. In terms of your network and the people whose lives you can touch by being connected, just go for it. Take every opportunity that presents itself to talk to the people you meet. There's not even any need to go to special networking events (which are largely overrated and take up precious time) as long as you react positively at this stage to anything that presents itself as you go about your job and your life.

The best thing about this approach? You should never feel alone or isolated as there will always be someone you can turn to for independent advice and direction. That's a very reassuring feeling, and don't forget to reciprocate as you progress in your own career.

Wishing you lots of luck … of your own making.

Beyond the Relationship Code Foundation

No matter what role or business you are in, everyone needs to understand the power and importance of making the most of every opportunity to interact and thereby build relationships. In the early years of your working life – the Foundation Years – if you do nothing other than this, you will be laying the foundation for a support network that can be with you into the future and will bring you unexpected opportunities. This is what this first Relationship Code book enables you to do.

Whether you are employed by a business, or have started your own, there will come a time when you need to do more than just use the power of everyday conversations. You'll want and need to start to take more control of situations and also guide conversations and relationships. During these Breakthrough Years, this will enable you to become recognised as an emerging leader. If you have your own business hopefully it is growing and your relationships both internally and externally will be a major factor in your overall success. How to do this will be covered in the second book in The Relationship Code series. Having understood and mastered the foundation elements, we will move on to reinforcing relationships, making them work for both parties and enabling you to make important things happen through these relationships.

Looking even further ahead, we have to think about how, with a strong network of connections that know, trust, understand and value us, we can have a profound impact on the business/business area we lead. You will be into your Leadership Years. In the third book in The Relationship Code series the focus is on winning business. If that immediately makes you think about having to sell, don't let that put you off. You will have gained all the core skills to do this via the earlier books. After all, whether you've realised it or not, the luck you'll have created for yourself will have come from enabling people to 'buy' you through the relationships you have been nurturing in your Foundation and Breakthrough Years. You'll simply be applying it much more proactively with a wider internal and external audience. You'll already know the principles and power of 'selling without selling' and you will be ready to take it to the expert level.

Businesses thrive and people grow when two parties choose to work together. That's true of internal relationships as well as external ones. It's the difference between someone choosing to buy, or buy in to, your services and engaging enthusiastically with you, rather than it feeling like a battle to achieve submission. In this expert stage, the key is about proactivity. As a leader in your business, the way you lead by example and demonstrate the ability to achieve results through relationships will be a catalyst to other to do the same. That way you will truly multiply your impact. That's what a great leader does – enables others to achieve their full potential.

Here's what your journey can look like.

Leadership Years
Multiplying the impact
of those around you
and proactively doing
good business through
your relationships

Breakthrough Years
Consciously and
confidently building
valuable sustainable
relationships to the
benefits of both parties

Foundation Years
Making the most of
every interaction

Your working life is an adventure with things to be discovered in terms of knowledge, capability and personal understanding. I hope we will be able to go on that journey together. May this book and the others in the Relationship

Code series be your companion and help you make it rewarding, enjoyable and lived in a way that makes you proud of what you do and how you do it.

I hope to hear from you via LinkedIn specifically and maybe other social media routes too. Connect with me when you have your account set up. I would be delighted to be a part of your network and hope I can also be part of your journey and success through sharing the power of the Relationship Code with you.

Q&A Index

1: Starting without any contacts _____ *11*

2: Making 'small talk' comfortable and interesting _____ *13*

3: Getting noticed in a crowd _____ *15*

4: Following up after an event _____ *17*

5: Handling untrustworthy people _____ *19*

6: Saying "No" _____ *21*

7: Approaching senior people _____ *23*

8: Asking great questions _____ *27*

9: Staying under control _____ *37*

10: Developing a business relationship after the first conversation _____ *40*

11: Giving difficult messages _____ *42*

12: Communicating succinctly _____ *46*

13: Expressing value to the other person _____ *49*

14: Getting clarity on expectations _____ *51*

15: Speaking at a seminar _____ *67*

16: Networking effectively _____ *70*

17: Making a meeting productive _____ *71*

18: Participation in a meeting _____ *75*

19: Describing what you do _____ *77*

20: Getting ready for an interview _____ *81*

21: Staying connected _____ *89*

22: Dressing for success _____ *93*